MW00785297

THE ULTIMATE GUIDE TO
GRAPPLING

THE ULTIMATE GUIDE TO
GRAPPLING

Compiled by Jon Sattler

Edited by Raymond Horwitz,
Jeannine Santiago, Jon Sattler and Jon Thibault

Graphic design by John Bodine

Front and back cover photos by Rick Hustead

©2007 Black Belt Communications LLC

All Rights Reserved
Printed in the United States of America
Library of Congress Control Number: 2007930257
ISBN-10: 0-89750-160-8
ISBN-13: 978-0-89750-160-6

First Printing 2007

BLACK BELT BOOKS
A Division of **OHARA ⬚ PUBLICATIONS, INC.**
World Leader in Martial Arts Publications

FOREWORD

From John Machado's Brazilian *jujutsu* to Hayward Nishioka's classical judo, from Gokor Chivichyan's hayastan system to Jim Wagner's reality-based combat, *The Ultimate Guide to Grappling* has everything the modern ground fighter needs to improve his game.

The effectiveness of grappling cannot be overstated. When MMA exploded into the mainstream, many were surprised by the number of matches that ended on the ground; even collegiate wrestlers who lacked the skills to finish by submission often dominated with takedowns and ground control. This confirmed what judo, jujutsu and *pankration* stylists knew all along—that grappling is a necessary weapon in every martial artist's arsenal. It has since become an evolutionary component in styles ranging from *kenpo* to *Krav Maga*.

We've scoured the *Black Belt* archives to bring you the quintessential grappling book, written by the world's foremost experts on the subject. Regardless of your level of expertise, *The Ultimate Guide to Grappling* will improve your ground game and serve as a valuable and entertaining reference tool.

CONTENTS

ISOTONICS AND JUDO
Uchikomi Training
by Hayward Nishioka • April 1969

*U*chikomi's repetitious, nonthrowing attack drills are among the finest ways to learn judo techniques. Almost every major competitor throughout the world uses uchikomi to improve his technique. When a competitor is practicing uchikomi, he will probably perform one of two kinds: static or dynamic.

In static uchikomi, one man stands erect while the other positions himself for a throw. He does this repeatedly without throwing his partner, who offers partial resistance to the attacker's entry.

In dynamic uchikomi, both the attacker and the defender move about in order to simulate *randori*. The attacker repeatedly enters and performs a technique up to the point of throwing him. The benefit of this type of practice is that the opponent is moving, whereas in static uchikomi, the opponent is standing still.

Regardless of the type of uchikomi used, there are many benefits that can be derived from it, including the following:

1. refines and trains reflexes
2. strengthens the muscles
3. promotes endurance
4. adds speed to your technique
5. instills confidence

Trained Reflexes

Charlie Chaplin made a movie called *Modern Times* that deals with how people are affected by mass production. His character is a worker in an automobile plant, and his only job is to tighten the nuts and bolts on a certain part of the car. Chaplin hilariously moves his arms, tightening the bolts with his wrenches. He does this all day long, six days a week. In his sleep, he still vigorously moves his arms like he's turning bolts. While this is an over-exaggeration of neuromuscular response, there is some truth to this. If anything, including a judo technique, is done repeatedly, it will become second nature.

Strengthens Muscles

In judo there is a saying:
Kimura no mae wa Kimura nashi,
Kimura no ato wa Kimura nashi.

Kazuo Shinohara is seen doing his uchikomi for tsuri komi goshi (propping up for a hip throw). In the sequences from 1 to 8, note how the technique is begun, ended and started anew—all with perfect form achieved with much practice.

Translated, this means "Before Kimura there was no Kimura; after Kimura there is no Kimura."

Masahiko Kimura is known as the strongest *judoka* ever. He won championship after championship with his famous one-arm shoulder throw, *ippon seionage.* For nine years, he consistently won the equivalent of the All Japan Championship, and he has no recorded losses. One of the ways

As Kimura once did, "trying to throw the tree" tenses all muscles and builds up strength for the hard pulls of judo. By placing the right elbow under the belt rather than by the belt, one can switch from a regular seionage to an ippon seionage uchikomi.

he would train: uchikomi.

Kimura would practice his uchikomi on a tree. He would wrap his belt around a tree and attempt to pull the tree out of the ground—roots, limbs, branches and all. He performed so many vigorous uchikomi that his back would become raw and bleed. Eventually, his back healed and became calloused. As for the tree, it's still standing, according to observers, but it has never looked the same. The tree's surface where Kimura would hit his back lost its rough bark. Where once stood an erect tree, now stands a crooked one. Even the ground around the tree had been altered by his heavy, scuffling feet.

By practicing uchikomi, he found that his hips and legs became much stronger and that it was easy to throw humans because they didn't have roots to hold them down. In the western world, this could be called an isometric exercise.

Endurance

Wind, stamina and endurance are all terms used to describe the capacity to withstand fatigue. In other words, when a person has stamina he doesn't poop out. He gets tough when the going gets tough!

Practicing against a tree can help develop an effective osotogari (outside major reaping technique) or a harai-goshi (sweeping loin technique), both important.

Here is a way to practice ashibarai (foot sweep). To improve speed in the sweep, a mattress or pillow tied around the trunk of the tree is advisable.

Trying to throw your opponent while another judoka holds onto your belt is an exercise in futility. But if you learn how to throw two people, one will be easier.

Uchikomi can be used to develop endurance. In Japan, it is common for college judokas to perform a few hundred nonstop. There are enthusiastic judokas who try to perform as many uchikomi perfectly without stopping. Some have even passed the 500 mark.

Speed

Kazuo Shinohara, a two-time U.S. judo champion, could throw an opponent so hard that he would be knocked unconscious when he hit the mat. Shinohara said, "Uchikomi practice is one of the best methods in building a strong, fast throw. With the practice of uchikomi, it was possible for me to cut down the amount of time that it took to enter into a technique."

When Shinohara first started practicing uchikomi, he could only perform a few a minute. Through constant practice, that number increased. Soon he could go into his technique in less than a second per try. In speeding up his ability, he achieved two things: One, he left his opponent less time to resist. Two, speeding up his *tsuri komi goshi* added more momentum to his throw.

With practice, anyone can build up to 60 uchikomi a minute. Of course these uchikomi should be performed perfectly. Anyone can do 60 sloppy uchikomi, but very few will take the effort to perfect their own technique.

Confidence

One definition of confidence reads: The state of mind characterized by one's reliance on himself or his circumstances; self-confidence. To add to this definition, confidence is a product of one's experience.

Our experience builds our confidence. If a person through his practice of uchikomi can enter into a *waza* (technique) in a split second, perform uchikomi on a big tree and shake the leaves from it, do a couple hundred uchikomi without stopping to rest, then uchikomi would increase any serious judoka's confidence.

An auto, like a human, can be moved (unlike the tree), thereby offering an offbeat way to "throw" a moveable object. This endeavor will develop strong hips and legs, both important.

15

THE PHYSICS OF JUDO

by Hayward Nishioka • Illustrations by Dave Enslow • December 1969

What are the factors of a good throwing technique? What makes a throw work one time and not work at another time? Why should the knees be bent when executing a major technique? Both beginning students and teachers ask these questions, so let's see if we can find some of the answers by studying five main factors that affect the application of major tournament techniques that utilize the hip in one way or another.

The Base of Support

Man's base of support is his feet. Stability is maintained when this base is neither too narrow nor too wide, and when the center of gravity is kept over the base of support. The object in most judo techniques is to catch the opponent off-guard just as he is about to re-establish a new base of support. Figures 1 and 4 place the *judoka* in an unstable position, vulnerable to attacks from any direction. This is because he has a small base of support. Figures 2 and 5 show two of the more acceptable stances with the feet spread apart just enough to keep one's balance. Figures 3 and 6 show extreme stances; Figure 3 is vulnerable to the sides where Figure 6 is vulnerable front and back.

Fig. 1   Fig. 2   Fig. 3   Fig. 4   Fig. 5   Fig. 6

Center of Gravity or Balance

The center of balance is located where body mass is divided equally. Normally, this spot is located somewhere in the lower abdomen. In Japan this spot is called *saika no itten*. Katherine Wells states in her book *Kinesiology* that the center of gravity is approximately 56 percent of a man's height and 55 percent of a woman's. In most situations that involve the hips, a trained technician will almost always place his hips below his opponent's. This action also enables him to place his center of gravity below his opponent's. If the opponent is shorter than the attacker or decides to bend his knees to lower his center of gravity, then it becomes necessary for the thrower to also bend his knees in order to get under the opponent.

Fig. 7   Fig. 8   Fig. 9

The Line of Gravity

The line of gravity is an imaginary line that passes through the body vertically from the head to the base of support (figures 10, 11). Equilibrium is lost when most of the body weight falls outside of the margin of this line (figures 12, 13).

In judo, it's easier to throw your opponent when you pull him outside of his line of gravity before applying the technique.

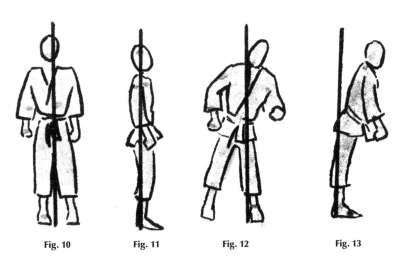

Fig. 10   Fig. 11   Fig. 12   Fig. 13

17

Levers

A lever is an instrument used to overcome a large amount of resistance with a small amount of energy. Basically, there are three types of levers, but for our purpose, we will only be concerned with one type: the first-class lever (figure 14).

The lever operates under three elements: (1) force, (2) axis or fulcrum and (3) resistance.

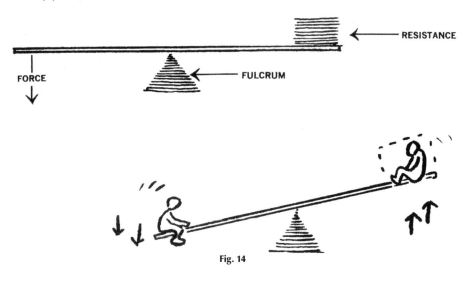

Fig. 14

Laws of Motion

Sir Isaac Newton, it seems, found out more than what we commonly hear tales about. Besides being hit on the head with an apple and stating the laws of gravity, he also stated a few other laws; laws which are applicable to the study of judo—the Laws of Motion:

1. Law of Inertia: An object at rest will remain at rest until acted upon by an external force.

2. Law of Acceleration: An object will change in velocity proportionate to the amount of force causing the change and inversely proportionate to the object's mass.

In football, if two athletes of almost equal weight run toward each other, the athlete who runs faster will usually cause more damage, even if he might be the lighter of the two. Here, the light athlete is able to compensate for his lighter weight by adding more momentum to his weight.

As in football, so it is with judo; speed can cause a change in the opponent's motion. If you can move into the correct position faster than your opponent can react to your action, then the chances of getting more throws per practices or per tournaments can be greatly increased.

The Five Factors

Fig. 15

Fig. 16

Combining these five factors, let's see how a throw works.

The use of judo techniques is often referred to as the use of leverage. Differing from what we would normally consider a lever, the judo lever is a vertical one; the resistance at the feet and the force applied at the top, near or on the head, the fulcrum lying somewhere between the two (figure 17).

Execution of a technique utilizing the hip becomes easier when the attacker's hips are placed on or below the opponent's center of gravity (figures 18, 19), and force is placed above the center of gravity. Both Eiji Maruki (1967 world champion) and Yasuhiko Nagatoshi (1967 U.S. grand champion) demonstrated this fact in the form of their low drop *seionage* in which their fulcrum was well below the opponent's center of gravity and in fact was hitting at the opponent's knees. If the fulcrum is placed above

19

FULCRUM

CENTER OF GRAVITY

RESISTANCE

Fig. 17　　　　　Fig. 18　　　　　Fig. 19

the center of balance, then the attacker must rely more on his strength and force to throw his opponent over.

Now, considering the line of gravity, Jiguro Kano states that it became easier to throw his teacher, Tsumetoshi Iikubo, when he would first pull him off-balance before applying the throw. He named this offbalanced position *kuzushi*. This state of being off-balance occurs when the opponent is pushed or pulled so far out of his line of gravity that he can no longer maintain equilibrium unless he re-establishes a new base of support (figures 20, 21, 22). It is often at this moment that the attacker has the best opportunity to enter into his technique. Entering at this time assures the thrower of knowing one thing: As long as he is in the right position, gravitational pull is on his side (figures 23, 24).

Much has been said about the off-balance position of the person to be thrown, but relatively little has been said about the balance of the thrower. In most major tournaments, it can be noted that the thrower is also in an off-balanced position. The thrower usually leans his body weight in the direction of the throw being executed. Note figures 25 and 26. This leaning action enables the thrower to utilize not only his arm strength, but also off-balanced weight to pull or push his opponent down for an *ippon*.

The placement of the base of support of the thrower will depend on strength and speed of the thrower and his opponent. If the thrower feels

This illustration shows how a small man can gain the advantage if his larger opponent is off-balance.

Fig. 20

that he need not enter deep and would rather rely on pulling his opponent to him, then he may do so. If on the other hand the thrower feels that his arms are no match with those of his opponent, then he should concentrate on his footwork and try to establish his base of support under his opponent's center of gravity. In some cases, competitors have been known to go under and even beyond this point.

Fig. 21

Fig. 22

Finally, speed in the application of a technique is an important factor, but it should not be placed before correct application procedures. Many times beginners and even advanced judo men will enter into a technique with a lot of speed but will not be able to throw their opponents. Perhaps this is because they are sacrificing correct application for speed and momentum. One should first learn the correct entry method, then build up on the speed of application (figure 27).

In keeping with the five factors of base of support, center of gravity, line of gravity, levers and laws of motion, see if you can tell where a technique has its flaws. See if you can correct your mistakes or help others objectively find their mistakes or bad habits. In doing so, you may come to realize the greatness of Dr. Kano's three maxims: (1) "maximum efficiency, minimum effort," (2) "self-improvement" and (3) "mutual welfare and benefit for all."

Fig. 23

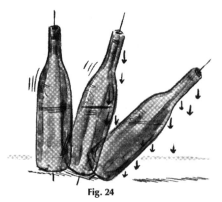

Fig. 24

Fig. 25

Fig. 26

Fig. 27

DANGER IN THE JUDO CHOKE?

by Ken Endow • April 1970

Reprint permission was granted from the Kodokan for its *Bulletin of the Association for the Scientific Studies on Judo, Kodokan, Report 1, "Physiological Studies on Choking in Judo"* and also from the USJF for the *1968 AAU-USJF Official Judo Handbook.*

His arms clamp around my throat. I fight with all my might, but within seconds, the ringing in my ears becomes deafening. The *dojo* spins and begins to fade away. Then, total blackness.

It takes only a moment to realize that I am on the mat, facedown.

I am certain only a half second has passed, but my opponent is waiting in the center of the fighting area, his judo *gi* neatly refolded and black belt retied. He's staring the confident glare of the victor. I must have been out for at least half a minute, possibly more.

My teammates told me that he knocked me out for the full count plus 20. It's hard to believe because I had jumped up, ready to defend myself, and felt prepared to continue the battle. But the match was over. *Ippon* was called. I lost.

How many *judoka* have experienced this sensation? The first time is spooky. Is it any wonder parents and physicians are among those most vehemently opposed to judo's choke hold?

Not knowing what happens to someone who is choked seems to be the main objection to choking, which *judoists* call *shime waza*. It was precisely this lack of knowledge that prompted the Kodokan Judo Institute to conduct a scientific study on the effects of choking. The experiments and the accompanying results were published by the Kodokan in a bilingual (Japanese and English) book called the *Bulletin of the Association for the Scientific Studies on Judo, Kodokan, Report 1, "Physiological Studies on Choking in Judo."*

A team of experts came together to discover whether there are any dangers in using shime waza. Representing several of Japan's foremost medical schools and universities as well as the Kodokan, this group of medical specialists and ranking educators used the electroencephalograph to detect brain changes, the earoxymeter for blood oxygen saturation, the sphygmomanometer for arterial blood pressure, the plethysmograph for peripheral blood vessel reaction and the micropipometer for skin temperature changes. Other studies probed the plasma protein concentration,

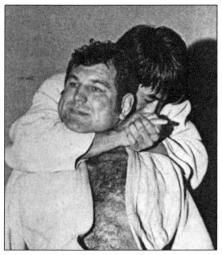

HADAKA-JIME
(BARE ARM CHOKE)

This is one of the easiest and fastest chokes to apply. As mentioned in the article, this choke can cause extreme pain. Since these findings were first published, revisions in the application of the choke have been introduced, making them more effective. Applying the choke, the attacker brings his right arm around the opponent's neck, slipping it underneath the chin of the victim. The radius bone of the attacker's arm must be wedged against the carotid artery. The attacker must keep his head tight against his opponent, forcing the victim to hunch over and bend into himself.

KATAJUJI-JIME
(ARM CROSS CHOKE)

One of the most commonly used chokes in competition is the katajuji-jime, and yet, it seems to be the most difficult to apply. The attacker begins the choke by facing his opponent and grasping the lapel with his left. Crossing the left and grabbing the opponent's right lapel with his right hand, the attacker inserts his thumb deep into the jacket and grasps a tight reign on the lapel. The opponent's lapel is used as a rope and is cinched tight across the opponent's left carotid artery, while the attacker's right arm is jammed into the right side of the opponent's neck.

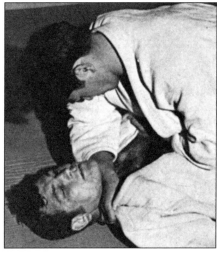

OKURIERI-JIME
(DEEP LAPEL CHOKE)

Grabbing the opponent by the lapel with the left hand and wedging the bare arm under the chin, this choke is applied by the attacker from the rear. As the opponent moves his right arm up to break the hold of the attacker's left hand on his lapel, the attacker comes from underneath the right armpit with his right, slipping between the shoulder and the nape of the neck, forcing the opponent's right arm up in the air and exerting pressure on the neck.

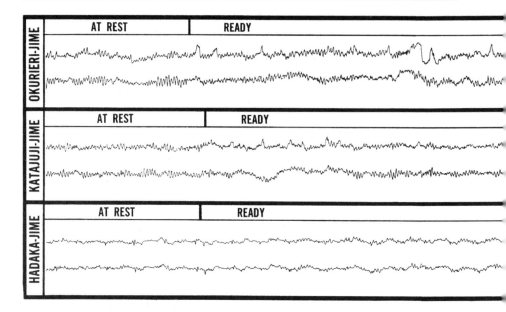

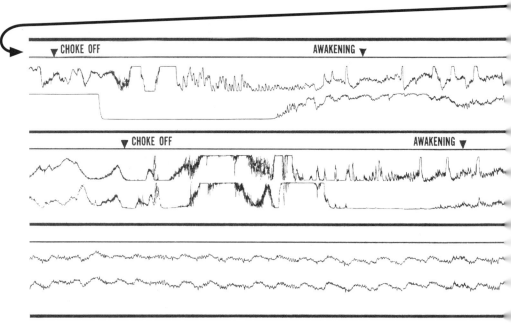

EFFECT OF CHOKING ON ELECTROENCEPHALOGRAM

Of the three types of chokes used in this experiment, the graph shows very little difference between the top two holds: okurieri-jime and katajuji-jime. The record of the subject on top shows a slight apprehension before the choke was on. On the bottom subject, records show a pattern signifying excruciating pain, but at no time does the person become unconscious.

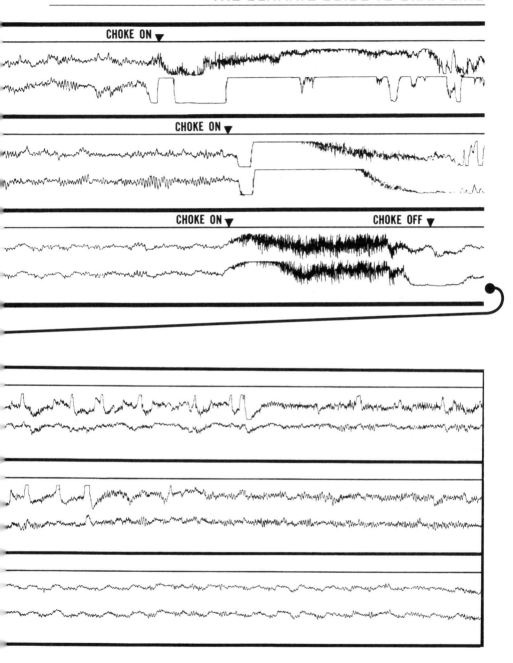

blood water volume, hematrocrit, complete blood count, eosinophil count and urine 17 ketosteroid content.

Scientific Search for Danger

Three other objectives of the study were to discover the different effects of the various choking methods, how long a choke affects the body and what causes the person to go unconscious.

Three methods of choking were used: *okurieri-jime,* the neck squeezed as a whole; *katajuji-jime,* the carotid arteries' region pressed; and *hadaka-jime,* the trachea depressed.

Dr. E. K. Koiwai said in the *1968 AAU-USJF Official Judo Handbook,* "Basically, except for one form of shime waza, hadaka-jime, the pressure is applied to the lateral side of the neck, which the anatomists call the carotid triangle. ... In the center of this triangle are the jugular veins, carotid artery and its branches, and the carotid sinus. No strong muscle protects this area.

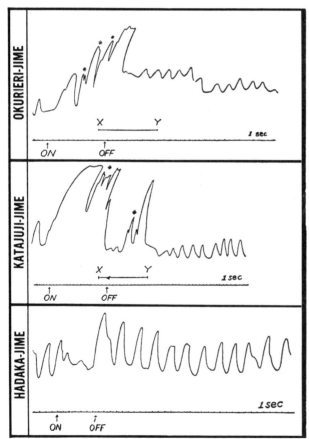

EFFECTS ON RESPIRATION
Convulsions are noted only on the top two charts by an asterisk mark. On the hadaka-jime choke hold chart, the subject has no convulsions and maintains consciousness throughout.

The pressure is applied in a certain manner, depending upon the technique, directly on these structures. It may be the fist or the collar of the judo gi. Very often it is the pressure of the distal end (joint) of the radius and the wrist that compresses the soft structures of the neck. Until the above name structures are sufficiently compressed, the choke will not be effective. The neophyte may submit not because of the choke but because of the fear of being choked or the pain produced by improper choking methods."

Koiwai wrote that the hadaka-jimi choke hold is different because part of the pressure is applied to the larynx and trachea, making it extremely painful. The opponent will usually submit before going unconscious. Before submitting, he will struggle harder because of the excruciating pain this hold causes.

Six high-ranking black-belt judoists were used for the Kodokan experiment. Five of them were victims while the sixth *dan* performed the designated chokes. Only in the katajuji-jime were the subjects, who laid on

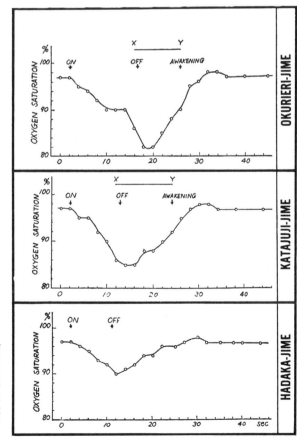

EFFECT ON OXYGEN SATURATION
Measuring the percentage of oxygen saturation in the blood of the helix of the ear with an earoxymeter, the top two choke holds show a marked drop in the amount of oxygen being absorbed, while the bottom graph shows only a slight decline.

a couch, strangled from the front. The two other chokes were performed from behind.

Once the equipment was checked and rechecked, the experiment was given the OK to commence. The sixth dan took his position and was given the signal to go ahead. The criterion for unconsciousness was the reflex dilation, or widening, of the pupils. The choker released his hold at the first sign of unconsciousness. Measurement of the eyes' pupils were made at rest, then at the ready position, and finally throughout the choking period until five minutes after regaining consciousness. The three chokes were performed on each of the five subjects, so 18 tests were recorded and analyzed.

After 10 seconds of choking, the victims fell unconscious. As soon as the subject was declared unconscious, the performer released him and the subject remained unconscious for 10 to 12 seconds. During this period, the victims sometimes developed clonus, a type of muscle spasm. All subjects woke up spontaneously. According to the *Bulletin*, the victims sometimes had dreams that were "not unpleasant" while they were unconscious. After awakening, the subjects did not complain about unpleasant feelings.

Hadaka-jime is too painful to induce unconsciousness and would be a poor method to rely on in tournament play because the opponent would probably struggle more to escape. However, with the okurieri-jime and the katajuji-jime, all the subjects lost consciousness and entered a similar state to sleeping. As the subject regained consciousness, his electroencephalogram readings returned to normal. It should be repeated that in all the cases, the performer released his grip immediately after the subjects fell unconscious, thereby limiting the effect of choking to a short period. But had the strangulation continued, serious aftereffects would be expected.

What causes unconsciousness from choking? The findings show that the stopping of the flow of blood to the head plays an important role in causing unconsciousness. In other words, the subject blacks out because of a lack of oxygen to the brain, which is fed blood through the carotid arteries.

Notes Epileptic Seizure

Also linked to the lack of oxygen to the brain are the convulsions that sometimes accompany a judo choke. The electroencephalograph recorded symptoms very similar to that of a short epileptic seizure.

To minimize risks, the Kodokan *Bulletin* advises judoka not to choke subjects with cardiac disorders or those suffering from hypertension because it increases blood pressure. It is also dangerous for youngsters because their central nervous systems and hearts haven't completely developed. The *Bulletin* emphasizes, however, that it is quite harmless for those trained in judo, although care must be taken not to continue the hold after the subject falls unconscious.

Since Jigoro Kano developed judo in 1882, there have been no reported deaths directly attributed to judo choking. Koiwai in the *1968 AAU-USJF Official Judo Handbook* attributes this remarkable record to four main reasons: Choking is supervised and observed by qualified, trained instructors and officials, the contestant submits before unconsciousness occurs, the contestant regains consciousness naturally and spontaneously without difficulty within 10 to 20 seconds of being choked out, and qualified instructors and officials prevent prolonged hypoxia (lack of oxygen to the body tissues) by immediate application of artificial respiration when necessary.

If the hold is released at the moment the victim becomes unconscious, the study shows that there are no serious side effects. With precautionary methods and qualified instructors and officials, choking techniques are a safe means of subduing an opponent in competition.

The biggest hurdle for the prospective choker is controlling the opponent's body because an experienced competitor will struggle vigorously to avoid being choked and because there are many techniques used to escape from a shime waza technique.

Not only is it safe when used correctly, but shime waza represents one of Kano's guiding principles: *sei ryoku zenryo* (maximum efficiency with minimum effort). When properly applied, the larger and stronger person can be subdued by the weaker and smaller opponent.

WHEN TWO THROWS ARE BETTER THAN ONE
Judo's Kouchigari-Ouchigari Combination
March 1973

This innovative judo technique is performed by former U.S. judo champion Hayward Nishioka. Using the *kouchigari* (minor inside reap) and the *ouchigari* (major inside reap) together, Nishioka (on the right) catches his opponent by surprise. This technique is reprinted from Nishioka's *Foot Throws: Karate, Judo and Self-Defense*.

(1) Assume a right natural grip and (2) force the opponent to his right by pulling on his right arm as you step back with your left foot. (3) Move into position for a kouchigari before the opponent tries to step forward. (4) Just as he is about to redistribute his weight to his right foot, reap that foot to his right, forcing him to lean on his left foot. (5) Quickly switch your reaping foot to his left foot, hooking him at the back of the knee. (6) Pull his left leg back and up, widening the gap between his feet, and then (7) drive forward with your hands and upper body. (8) Maintain your grasp until you have forced him onto his back.

THE ART OF THE UKE

by David Orange Jr. • Illustrations by Richard Moncrief • July 1981

*A*ikido techniques inspire onlookers to gasp, gawk and say, "Gee, I wish I could throw somebody like that!" The *tori* gets the glory, while the *uke* is lucky to roll to a humble stance on yonder side of the mat.

The tori and uke are designations often used in throwing arts, such as aikido and judo. The tori performs the throw, and the uke, who usually initiates the action, takes the fall. Actually, the tori and uke are "not one, not two," like the *yin-yang*. To most observers, the tori is the more obvious partner and the more desirable role to play. But the art of the uke is every bit as vital and necessary as that of the tori, and it may even be more useful in self-defense.

Properly approached, the art of the uke performs at least three functions: It protects the uke from injury, it forces the tori to be honest, and it allows the uke to overcome and become tori.

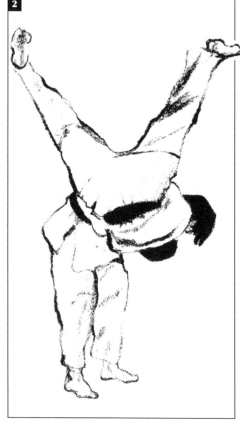

The first function—breaking falls—is obvious: Everyone knows that the uke takes the fall. This is an oversimplification of the uke's role, but it is the foundation of the art as a whole.

The uke's main tool is *ukemi*—a series of techniques for dissipating the shock of a fall to lessen the odds of injury. The most common ukemi are the rolls of aikido and the flat falls often used in judo. Other varieties include the one-foot ukemi of the *yoseikan*, adapted for use on rough terrain, and the vertical diving method, which lowers the body smoothly with both arms from a position similar to a handstand.

While he is being thrown, the uke must exhale smoothly, strongly and continuously. Breathing is a core spiritual practice of *budo*, and the sooner breath/body coordination is sought in any art, the sooner real progress will be made.

When falling, proper breathing helps the uke remain relaxed, relying on the tori to neither drop the uke straight onto the mat nor leave the uke

The yin-yang of the tori and uke: The tori (the thrower) prepares a seionage (shoulder throw) (1). Even while in the air (2), the uke can opt to roll with the throw. This roll by the uke creates a tighter throw than the tori intended (3) unbalancing him and allowing the uke to roll through (4), coming out on top.

unmoved. The uke should not fall simply because the tori moves, and here we reach the second part of the uke's art: keeping the tori honest.

In aikido, more than judo, practice partners sometimes cooperate too much. Minoru Mochizuki—founder of yoseikan budo, an art that combines aikido and judo—calls this negotiation. While it may result in spectacular-looking throws, he maintains that it is cheating. It may happen when both the tori and uke openly agree to do it, or when the uke unconsciously believes he is expected to fall down. In the latter case, the uke practically throws himself in anticipation of the technique. Experienced tori should recognize this and discourage it because it robs everyone of the chance to evaluate and respond to realistic scenarios.

The responsible uke will "grab him for good," as Mochizuki says, or at least attempt to gain control. The uke is, after all, not a dummy to be thrown around at will but should convincingly represent a real attacker. *Aikidoka* sometimes get so hypnotized by the cleverness of their own techniques that they refuse to respect the uke—and therefore any attacker—as a strategist and fighter.

This is not to suggest that the uke become rigid and obstinate. Knowing when to give up, either by *maitta* (tap out) or falling, is essential. But he should not fall too easily. The uke should strive to keep his balance, even while making his attack.

If he is grasping, the uke should approach with authority, like a police officer making an arrest. He doesn't merely swan dive for the tori's wrist but attacks from a position of balanced strength, with the intention of doing something definite to the tori. Likewise, a striking attack must be carried out without intentionally overextending to throw himself off-balance. This is not a help to the tori, and the tori should discourage it.

To attain this level, one must master the basic ukemi. When a skilled tori receives an attack of realistic energy and responds with true *aiki* or *ju*, then a powerful throw can result, and the uke must rely on sharp reflexes to survive the fall. In fact, without strong attacks, the tori can never develop true aikido.

Mochizuki studied judo with Jigoro Kano and aikido with Morihei Uyeshiba, and he stresses that the uke can be very strong. "Between two well-trained opponents," he says, "a punch, a kick or a throw will have little effect, and the strongest one on the ground will win." If nothing else, the uke may be able to drag the tori down with him in a real situation and defeat him through grappling. Therefore, Mochizuki includes extensive mat work in his training.

This is not because of any disrespect that he holds for aikido. Rather, he knows that an opponent skilled at the art of the uke will be extremely difficult to overcome. Continual falling and rising, coupled with educated practice habits, builds great endurance. Also, a subtle uke can actually switch places with the tori and throw him. This is done through *sutemi waza*, or sacrifice techniques, in which the uke uses the momentum of his own fall to unbalance the tori and throw him.

Yoseikan is usually among aiki styles in that it teaches a broad repertoire of sutemi waza and half-sutemi waza. For an example of *sutemi* by reversal, imagine the common judo technique of *seionage*: over-the-shoulder throw.

Both players strive to maintain balance, but one is quicker and takes the advantage. At this point, he would be designated the tori.

As the tori sets up for seionage, the uke can recognize his dire straits and opt to go with the flow. Thus, as the tori reaches the full sweep of his power drive, the uke has merged with the motion, twisting his own torso around further and faster than the tori had intended.

This creates centripetal force, drawing the tori into an orbital arc around the falling uke. If done tightly and naturally enough, this strategy can unbalance the tori, causing him to fall. In this case, the tori's own ukemi must be up to par, for he will absorb all the shock of the double throw, winding up as the uke.

If properly executed, this escape from seionage will place the new tori in an advantageous position for *atemi* or a holding technique.

Anyone who seeks to become a great tori should work on falls and encourage strong, realistic attacks. A humble responsibility, the art of the uke not only makes practice possible but also lifts all players to greater truths of martial practice.

COUNTER-THROWS IN JUDO

by John Earl Maberry • Photos by Vince Volker • Techniques posed by J.B. Gross of the Philadelphia Judo Dojo • March 1982

The first thing to know in judo about countering a throw is this: If you have to stop and think about what counter to use, you're already too late. Countering is a part of grappling, which demands that the conscious, thinking mind takes a back seat to the reflexes of the subconscious. When the time available for defense is measured in split seconds, the ponderous process of conscious thought becomes a dangerous and often self-defeating burden.

The general rule in learning how to counter throws, as with any aspect of close-quarters combat, is: Drill the technique so frequently, so thoroughly, so exhaustively that the reflexes trigger movement out of instinct rather than an active, thoughtful command.

The concept is derived from *mushin-no-shin* or "mind of no mind," a

Leg Technique: Often the counter-technique is the same as the technique being used to attack. Such is the case with osotogari (major outside reap). The tori comes in hooking hard for his osotogari (1), establishing his secure two-hand grab. The uke merely lifts his own leg and clips back (2) to hook the tori's attacking leg. As he does this, he shifts his weight forward to overbalance the tori. From there, it's a simple osotogari (3).

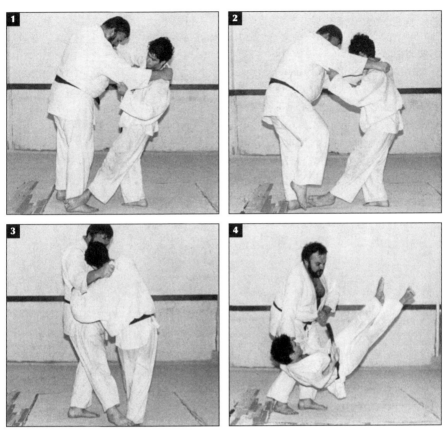

Leg Technique-Sweep: Countering a sweep is never easy, unless one relaxes and lets the subconscious do the hard work. To illustrate: The tori (the thrower) comes in with a sasae-tsuri-komi-ashi (lifting-pull throw with supporting foot). And the uke lifts his foot in a small counterclockwise circle, letting the tori's foot slide by (1-2). Immediately, he applies a sasae-tsuri-komi-ashi of his own (3), guiding his opponent to the mat (4) with a hard pull on the rear of the collar.

Japanese maxim referring to action without thought—that is, reflexive action. It is an invaluable concept to any serious martial artist. Without it, he is only as good as his ability to think and transmit his thoughts into action.

To develop this mushin-no-shin for use in judo or other forms of grappling, one must take a slow, often tedious route. First, one must diligently practice his own techniques so frequently that he can use them with ease, comfort and facility. Then he must begin to consider and assess the options open in various defensive situations.

J.B. Gross of Philadelphia—one of the most prominent judo and *jujutsu* instructors—said, "If a man is doing a hip technique, he has to turn his back on you. As soon as he turns his back, you have a couple or three options open to you. By working through these options slowly with a partner, you can explore the methods that work best for you. There's not one rule for all counters to hip techniques. It depends on the type of hip technique he's using; it depends on his size, body weight and grip; it depends on your own balance—whether you might want to counter with the same move, whether you might have to roll with it and try to use the throw to pull him to the mat. ... There's a lot to consider."

But all this consideration must happen in the long hours of training, not in the split second between the beginning of a throw and the oppor-

Hip-Throw Attack: The tori leads off with a right uchimata (1-2). As he comes in, the uke lowers his weight to secure his posture and ruin the balance of the throw attempt. He secures a two-handed grab on the tori and hauls him off the mat (3) with a high lift to the left rear corner, arching his spine in order to properly support the added weight. Immediately, he pivots to one side and drops the tori (now the uke) with a controlled drop (4).

Hand Technique: Sometimes a technique is best countered by another throw of similar type. In case of the seionage (back carry throw), try te waza (hand throw). As the tori sets up for a seionage to defend against a choking arm wrap (1), the uke performs a tai-sabaki (turning movement), keeping the tori's elbow close to his side (2), and continues the motion rearward. Thus, the attacker is thrown backward and down to the mat (3).

tunity to counter. When drilling for this, one should put oneself through as many situations as possible: a larger opponent, a smaller opponent, a taller opponent, a squat opponent, an opponent who is highly skilled at a given throw, an opponent who is not as skilled and so on.

"If the man is coming in on a driving leg technique," Gross continues, "where you'd have to breakfall backward—you have to start thinking about pivoting. If, say, he comes in with a right side major inside reap, you'll have to pivot to the left. If he's doing a minor inside reap, it's just the opposite. For leg sweeps, you have to know that to do a proper leg sweep, your opponent has to be moving. So to determine a counter for that, you have to start out moving, giving the other guy a chance to start his sweep so that you can do a realistic counter. Anybody can counter a foot sweep if he is standing still with good balance."

To realistically develop one's counter-techniques, one must train realistically. The *randori* (training partner) must earnestly try to perform his throw so that the defender will have to develop counters that really work,

Matwork and Pins: Yokoshiho-gatame (side four corners hold) is a common and very tough pin to get out of. The Yokoshiho-gatame is applied (1). The defender turns (2), keeping his right elbow in the pit of the opponent's stomach, and reaching over with his left arm, he grabs his foe's belt. He pulls the opponent's left leg as close as he can to his own head and pulls him to his own left corner (3).

not ones that only work under ideal conditions. Otherwise, one's defenses will be almost totally useless.

In judo there are scores of throws, and there are dozens more in other grappling arts around the world. Developing workable counters to each will take years, not days, of mat work. And once a counter has been developed to work against a certain type of opponent, there is no guarantee it will work against other kinds of opponents. This is why many judo instructors suggest training with as many different kinds of opponents as possible. It is preferable to deal with foes who are larger, stronger and more highly skilled in throwing. In this way a deeper, more profound understanding of countering will be achieved.

THE SECRET TO JUDO THROWS
Training Tips to Improve Your Skill

by Charles S. Brocato and Kathryn E. King • Photos courtesy of Charles S. Brocato • April 1988

The object of a judo throwing technique is to throw your opponent without being thrown yourself. Many practitioners, however, succeed only in throwing themselves because they haven't been taught what to do if their opponent departs from the expected response.

Too many *judoka* think there is only one correct way to perform a throw, so they study and teach this method and ignore any alternatives. In reality, judo is a dynamic art that's meant to be experimented with and adapted to different positions, heights and strengths, and to varying personal styles.

This article will examine three related throws, along with training methods and attitudes that will help the student make these throws a part of his

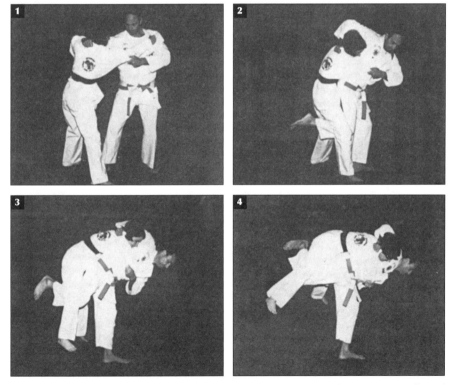

To perform uchimata (inner thigh throw), the judoka should grab (1) the back of his opponent's collar and pull his adversary forward by the sleeve. The judoka then back-pivots into his foe, bringing (2) his right leg up between his opponent's legs. The judoka bends over (3) and raises his reaping leg in unison with the body, lifting the opponent into the air while maintaining his grip on his adversary. The final step (4) is to catapult the opponent into the throw by thrusting the body and leg forward.

mind and body. Once the student understands the principles underlying these techniques, he is more capable of adapting them to any situation.

Haraigoshi, hane-goshi and *uchimata* are grouped in *tachi waza,* or throws done from a standing position. Haraigoshi and hanegoshi are *koshi waza* (hip or loin techniques), while uchimata is an *ashi waza* (foot or leg technique). Although they belong to two separate groups, these three techniques can be conveniently taught together because the body dynamics are from similar positions.

The following training tips will help you master these throws.

As you enter the mat area, think about the force in your body when you pull your partner hard with your arms. Contemplate the "lift-pull" and raising your partner's leg from the mat as you drive in for the throw. Judo practitioners benefit from spending time moving each other in *tai-sabaki* (turning action), a smooth, circular motion, not jerky. Practice this until

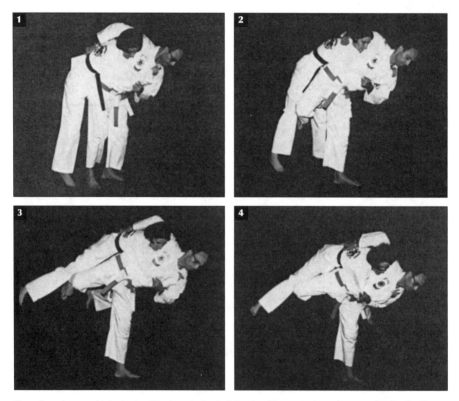

To perform hanegoshi (springing hip throw), the judoka should step (1) in such a way that his back is to the opponent's front and his leg is off-center to the leg he is going to reap. The judoka then raises (2) his reaping leg and pulls strongly on the opponent's sleeve and belt (or collar), lifting his foe into the air. The opponent is locked into a throwing position (3), and the judoka simply needs to twist his body and catapult (4) his adversary forward.

you experience the "lift" created by centrifugal force, which will occur when you create a null vector. Creating a null vector means you have canceled the force of your opponent's motion by helping him travel in the direction he was moving in, only faster than he expected.

The creators of judo realized that a smaller, weaker person could use the movement of a larger, stronger opponent to gain an advantage. By going with and moving faster than the opponent, the smaller person could cancel out the opponent's strength. Even the largest, toughest adversary feels intimidated when he suddenly finds himself toppled hard onto his backside.

The early judo masters knew nothing about vectors, but they learned through practice that certain ways of directing body movements brought about certain results.

Hanegoshi, haraigoshi and uchimata all depend on the student's willingness to turn his back—a vulnerable position—and use his leg, while at the same time applying a powerful pull to unbalance and set up the opponent. This is the hardest lesson to teach and to receive in judo. Students may never quite lose that initial fear of turning their backs on their adversary. In judo, you must learn to let go in order to achieve. By paying strict attention to the precepts of judo, one can learn a lot about life—he learns to let go of fear.

Practice turning your back and applying a powerful pull on your partner at every opportunity, and drive forward with all the technique at your command. Losing the fear of turning your back does you no good if you wind up getting thrown every time because your technique is poor.

Some students think they can bypass technique by utilizing brute strength. This can be done, if you are strong enough, but it ignores the principles of judo and, hence, makes you work a lot harder than necessary. The perfect combination is technique and power.

A student may believe he has learned to turn his back yet wonder why he still can't achieve a smooth uchimata. All too often, his instructor can't understand it, either, and he may berate the student when the problem actually lies with the instructor. This type of instructor often hasn't emphasized strongly enough, by word and demonstration, that the student must be the player, not the spectator.

You cannot play two parts while you are engaged in *randori* (judo sparring). You can't be both player and spectator at the same time. When you turn your back and drive forward for uchimata, you can't be looking back at your opponent. Don't watch your throw to see how it is going. Instead, look where you are going to throw your opponent, not from whence you

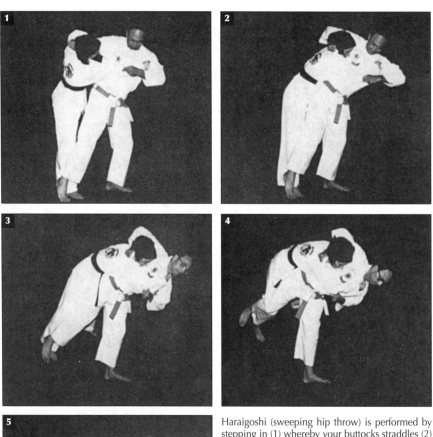

Haraigoshi (sweeping hip throw) is performed by stepping in (1) whereby your buttocks straddles (2) the thigh you intend to sweep. Pull the opponent hard into your body, lean forward (3) and use your right foot to reap (4) the opponent to the outside of his leg that is parallel to your buttocks. Continue with the leg in an upward fashion and topple him (5) over your hip by twisting your body.

came. Your opponent will tend to follow the line of action if your technique is executed correctly. If you look back, you tend to split your forces.

Too many instructors and students foster the idea that it is bad to be thrown. Consequently, the students guard against being thrown in class. They must let go of the fear of being thrown, the fear of losing, the fear of embarrassment. This will set one free for the bigger contest—life. By being thrown, you learn, in a unique way, that specific throw every inch of the way down, teaching you awareness in its finest form. Teaching caution is good—but it should be communicated as awareness, not as fear of defeat.

Little by little, one learns to let go and develop the true technical aspect of judo. At the same time, its spirit comes through to serve him in good stead in everything in life. Possessing discipline without an understanding of what and how this discipline is being achieved serves only to undo the student. He can become extremely disciplined, but without understanding, he can become self-aggrandizing in that discipline.

Approach the mat with an attitude of calmness. First study the pattern of the throw, work the throw. Then, in order to learn how to feel the force of the throw, you must learn not to think of the throw as you attempt to do it. You must become the throw. This builds fluidity of motion, balance and confidence without ego involvement.

You must never enter the mat thinking, as some are taught, "I must demolish this opponent. I hate this man." This type of thinking leads to exhaustion physically as well as psychologically. This negative energy comes from the spirit, goes to the mind and manifests through the physical. If the mind is stressed with a particular ideal or pattern, this energy cannot flow smoothly and generate the best pattern, because the mind is the builder.

Another way of looking at it: Spirit, mind and body must function as one in order to produce the finest judo. This concept is seldom taught anymore. The film *Star Wars* pointed out this principle very succinctly. When Luke Skywalker was advised near the end of the movie to "Let go. Use the force," he was able to switch off the targeting computer he was depending on and believe in his own abilities. Through this belief and expectancy, he functioned as one unit. The physical wasn't fighting the mind, and the mind wasn't fighting the spirit.

This is what judo or any martial art is all about. The same concept may be applied to anything in life. However, all too often we see that the judoka is possessed by the throw because his approach to it is primarily physical in nature. To become a true *judoist,* one must possess the throw and not allow the throw to possess him.

HAPKIDO'S SCIENCE OF THROWING
Six Principles Vital to Good Technique
by John Earl Maberry • Photos by Robert Clark Jr. • April 1990

Throwing techniques are a part of nearly every martial art and are the cornerstone of styles such as judo, *jujutsu, aikido* and *hapkido.*

A throw is a powerful weapon, a difficult skill to master and an exciting spectacle to watch. By using a throwing technique, a fighter can manipulate someone more than twice his own size or he can throw one opponent into another when attacked by multiple assailants. Throws can cripple or kill, or they can be delivered with a featherlike touch. They are useful as self-defense techniques or can serve as the core of an endurance workout.

Throws are as old as combat. They appear in the ancient Indian art of *vajramushti*, Greek and Roman wrestling, kung fu, French *savate* and even the most modern forms of karate. They are easy to execute when you know the proper technique but are also astoundingly easy to get wrong. A bad throw can do more damage to the thrower than the opponent.

Hapkido is a Korean interpretation of jujutsu and a direct descendant of *daito-ryu aikijujutsu*. Like its parent system, hapkido uses a tremendous amount of throws. By the time a practitioner reaches first degree black belt, nearly every technique he attempts ends with a throw or takedown. In hapkido, throws are as essential as locking techniques. Most of the art's hand strikes and kicks are structured to weaken an opponent's balance so that he may be taken down or to allow the *hapkidoist* to get close enough to execute a throw.

One of hapkido's core concepts is the water principle, which teaches total penetration of the opponent's guard. In using the water principle, the hapkidoist theoretically surges through the opponent's guard and engages the enemy from close quarters. Strikes and kicks are vital, but grappling skills are the fundamental weapon of hapkido.

To execute a throw correctly, the practitioner has to look deeper than the move itself. Throws are one of the most scientific aspects of the martial arts; they rely entirely on physics. The most important throwing principles are mass manipulation and torsion, leverage, impetus and force, commitment and gravity, posture, and circularity. Once he gains an understanding of these principles, the practitioner must then prepare for the rigors of full-speed, full-power grappling. All preparation begins with a two-pronged approach: physical conditioning and breakfall training.

The body must be able to absorb a tremendous amount of impact when practicing throws, especially at the beginner level. Students will be able to diminish the impact with better breakfall skills.

Breakfalls are best learned in class from a knowledgeable instructor because there are countless possible mistakes that can ruin the breakfall and cause serious injury. After a student has spent several months conditi-

By grabbing the opponent's belt, or any other clothing, the hapkido stylist can add lifting power and impetus to the throw, literally whipping the opponent off the ground.

By committing to the pull of gravity during a throwing maneuver, the hapkido stylist is also carrying his opponent's mass along with him, however unwilling the opponent might be.

tioning and strengthening his body, he can begin practicing breakfalls at an advanced level. One method of learning the breakfall is the two-hand somersault, whereby the student performing the fall uses a light hand-press on his partner's back to direct the speed and angle of his breakfall and then commits himself entirely to the movement.

Physical Principles

To understand the science of throwing, you have to take the technique from the beginning, encountering the principles as the need for them appears.

• *Mass manipulation and torsion.* The grip used to hold, pull, push and lift the opponent is a key element. With a proper grip, the thrower can employ "torsion" to manipulate the opponent's weight and body mass. Torsion is the rapid twisting of mass on its axis. In simpler terms, imagine

Throwing is an art of circles and arcs. One example of this principle of circularity is the "fireman's carry," in which the thrower's body serves as an axle, wheeling the opponent around it.

an invisible line that begins at the tip of the skull and goes straight down through the body until it touches the ground between the feet. By holding onto an opponent with both hands, the opponent is "torqued" by pulling sharply in with one hand as the other hand pushes out with equal force. The effect is that the opponent's body spins with speed and ease. Torsion does not take strength as much as it takes surprise and speed.

• *Leverage.* Once the player has seized the advantage and begun his throw, he has to place his feet, spine and body in the position most conducive to a good throw. This placement varies with each throw, sometimes radically. However, certain factors should be considered in every throw. For example, because the hip is often used to lift the opponent, it has to be placed at a level that will allow the thrower to pull the opponent's weight against, onto and eventually over it. This necessitates placing the thrower's hip lower than the opponent's. Various types of crouches allow this kind of tactical positioning, and it will vary from throw to throw.

• *Impetus and force.* The thrower has to apply force in order to create the impetus that starts the opponent's body moving, encourages it to cooperate with the throw and redirects it to the ground. Muscular strength is important but not Herculean strength. A person of average size and build can perform as powerful a throw as a larger, more muscular person as long as he relies on science rather than brute strength. The difference comes in how the person's available strength is exploited. For example, if a person torques someone as he pulls him forward, he will get the opponent's weight moving at a respectable rate of speed without using raw strength. Torsion accelerates mass, and tilting that torsion allows gravity to assist in manipulation. Tilt that weight over and you have fast lift. Torque the fulcrum and you have redirection of mass in one of its most powerful states. There are even tricks that can be used to accelerate the lift and add more power to the throw.

One such trick is the "floating leg." The hapkido stylist torques his opponent and pulls him onto his hip. He accelerates the speed of the lift by tensing the muscles of his right buttock and lifting his right leg in a sharp rear rising kick. The buttock muscles are so strong that they will lift the entirety of an opponent's weight with ease. Aside from achieving a faster lift and throw, this floating leg trick also tilts the opponent into his descent quicker and more smoothly, avoiding possible collisions with the hapkidoist's standing leg.

A variation of this technique uses a grab to the opponent's clothes or belt to add extra impetus and literally whip the opponent off the ground.

The "floating leg" technique, in which the hapkido stylist torques the opponent and pulls him onto his hip, is one method of increasing the effect of leverage in a throw.

This is why a good breakfall technique is so important: A throw can reach upward of 60 miles an hour.

• *Commitment and gravity.* Force and velocity are also affected by the amount of physical commitment to the throw. While it is dangerous to commit one's entire body to a punching or kicking technique, such is not the case with a throw. Once the opponent has been lifted and the throw has begun, the thrower moves his own weight forward toward the floor. By committing to the pull of gravity, the hapkidoist is also carrying his opponent's mass along with him, however unwilling the opponent might be. While his opponent can do nothing to halt the process, the hapkido stylist can use his support leg to shift back to an upright position once his adversary is totally committed to the pull of gravity.

Breakfalls are best learned in class from a knowledgeable instructor because there are countless possible mistakes that can cause the practitioner serious injury.

Gravity is the thrower's ally, but it requires that he offer his victim up to its pull. If the opponent's balance and support have not been completely disrupted, the opponent can shift his weight and escape gravity's pull, and he can even use the improperly directed force to counter-throw his foe.

• ***Posture.*** The posture of the thrower at the end of the technique is as important as his posture before and during the throw. The dangers of poor post-throw posture are many: injuries to the feet, knees, spine, lower back, arms, face, groin and head. It is considered best to end a throw with some variation of the horse stance; such a posture keeps the opponent checked in close, limiting his counterfighting options while allowing the thrower to deliver his finishing techniques. Hapkido throws almost always end with a finishing strike, usually executed as the opponent is hitting the ground. The double-shock effect is devastating.

• *Circularity.* Throwing is an art of circles and arcs. There is no such thing as a linear throw, because at least one major joint (hips, knees, shoulders, etc.) has to rotate in order to manipulate mass. To try and displace an opponent's mass in a straight line would result in a shove or a straight lift, neither of which are throws.

The circle also allows the opponent's weight to be directed toward and around an obstacle, as with the hip lever mentioned earlier. A simple leg reap uses a crescent-type kick and angular tilt of the hips to execute the throw. A hip throw wheels the opponent over a tilted and rotating hip.

A more dramatic example of the circle is seen in the stomach throw. In this throw, the hapkidoist places one foot on the opponent's groin or bell and then collapses his own weight into a tight, sitting ball, submitting entirely to the pull of gravity. Because of the hapkido stylist's firm grip on his jacket, the opponent is pulled forward so sharply that he is likewise caught in the unbreakable pull of gravity.

* * *

There is a saying among serious hapkidoists that the goal of studying the art is to become a "combat scientist." Certainly, throwing is a scientific technique, not some secret or mystical maneuver done with mirrors. It is probably safe to say that there are no real secrets in the martial arts, nor should there be. If martial artists have to rely on secrets in order to accomplish the task of self-defense, they have missed something somewhere along the way.

Fighting skill comes from rigorous training and in-depth study. Performance alone is not enough; knowledge of how and why something works is the best weapon. An educated fighter can find a way to overcome an opponent who lacks education. The basics of physics are actually quite simple and become even more so when one learns how to take a technique apart and explore how it functions. This is true of kicking, punching and blocking, and most certainly of throwing.

ROYCE GRACIE'S SECRET WEAPON
Brazilian-Jujutsu Takedown Techniques
by David Meyer • Photos courtesy of David Meyer • November 1994

The popularity of Brazilian *jujutsu* skyrockets every time Royce Gracie steamrolls another challenger at the Ultimate Fighting Championship. Gracie, 27, won the first two UFC tournaments and is undefeated in seven bouts at the event. What is his secret? What fighting techniques have allowed him to defeat bigger and stronger opponents time and time again?

In the following article, *Black Belt* examines some of the Brazilian-jujutsu techniques and strategies Gracie has used in his bouts and takes you onto the mat with members of the Machado jujutsu family, several of whom have trained with Gracie family members and know their tactics.

One Punch, No Kill

The biggest question confronting a martial artist who wants to add ground-fighting skills to his arsenal is, How can I take a good fighter off his feet and live to tell about it? The Machados—who operate two jujutsu schools in Southern California—have learned from experience that it is possible to force a clinch and take down even a highly skilled stand-up fighter. This is because landing a single fight-stopping blow on a moving opponent is difficult, even more so when that opponent is a grappler trained to close the fighting distance.

Even if you are completely unskilled at closing the distance, you have a good chance of avoiding your opponent's intended knockout blow and forcing him into a clinch. Just watch a boxing or kickboxing match, and you will see that competitors who trade blows while intentionally remaining in punching range are not frequently knocked out by a single decisive punch. The issue for the grappler is not risking a knockout punch but avoiding unnecessary blows while entering for the clinch.

A good grappler always tries to remain out of prime striking range until the moment of entry. Your opponent wants to strike you, but as a grappler, you don't want to strike him. You want only to pass through striking range at the right moment to clinch him. This means that, instead of the usual cat-and-mouse game to set up a good finishing blow, he has very few chances to seriously hurt you as you charge in and attach yourself to his body.

"The opponent has only one chance to knock me out; otherwise he's mine," John Machado says. "If he doesn't connect, I'll be in. I have never seen one strike finish a street fight against someone skilled in jujutsu."

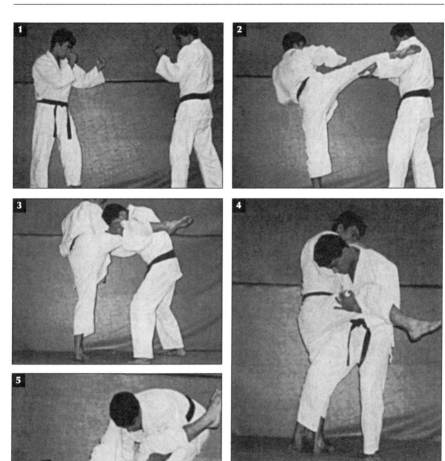

Attempting a kick against a Brazilian-jujutsu stylist can be dangerous, as seen here. Two fighters face off (1), and one attempts (2) a roundhouse kick that is captured by the Brazilian-jujutsu stylist. As he traps (3) the leg, the jujutsu practitioner moves in close and places (4) his foot behind his opponent's foot in preparation for a leg sweep that sends (5) his adversary to the ground.

Closing the Fighting Distance

The first step in closing the fighting distance is to stay out of the "danger zone." Measure the danger zone by having a partner extend his arm and make a fist. You then do the same and move until your fist touches his. This is the optimal distance for a grappler because it gives you enough space to react to most attacks, and it is short enough so you can easily traverse it on the way to the clinch. Note that a good stand-up fighter can cross greater distances by using footwork or jumping attacks, but these long-distance techniques give you even more time to react.

An opponent's weight usually shifts to his front leg after he throws a punch or kick, and when his weight is on his front foot, he cannot use it to strike. Therefore, closing the distance immediately after he punches or kicks raises the odds of an easy clinch.

Try to close the distance when your opponent is slightly off-balance. This way, he has an even smaller chance of landing a solid blow. Remember, the key is not to avoid being touched; it is to avoid being hit hard or knocked out. Assuming you enter at the wrong time and he actually throws a powerful strike, the chances of that blow landing squarely and stopping you are slim. Most often, the blow glances off its target, and you can still force the clinch.

Distraction Techniques

Distraction techniques can facilitate your entry into grappling range. Perhaps the most simple distraction maneuver is a knee stomp. Use your forward leg to attempt a stomping kick to your opponent's closest knee. As he attempts to avoid the kick, place your leg back on the floor and quickly move in. Whether the stomping technique lands is not important. What is important is that you commit to the technique, so even if the opponent withdraws his knee, you have stepped in and closed the fighting distance.

Another distraction maneuver is a quick flick of the hands toward your opponent's eyes. This causes him to momentarily raise his guarding hands. Begin to penetrate the instant after you flick your hands while your adversary is still reacting to the attempted eye strike.

Avoid the common entry error of dropping your head and lurching forward with your arms outstretched. Such approaches do not allow you to see where you are going. If your opponent backpedals and angles off to one side, you will charge past him like a bull and miss the opportunity to close the gap. Another problem is that your hands are not available to protect your face because they are too far out in front of you. This makes you a prime target for a rising knee strike to the head. Yet another problem is that, if you succeed in grabbing the opponent with your hands, your body is so far away you cannot properly control him for a safe takedown.

When you close the fighting distance, remember to hold your hands high and angle your body to minimize your vulnerability. If you accidentally move in as your opponent throws a strike, use your arms and body to parry the blow and keep moving forward. For example, if he throws a jab as you enter, use your palm to parry the blow across your head and

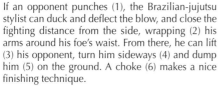

If an opponent punches (1), the Brazilian-jujutsu stylist can duck and deflect the blow, and close the fighting distance from the side, wrapping (2) his arms around his foe's waist. From there, he can lift (3) his opponent, turn him sideways (4) and dump him (5) on the ground. A choke (6) makes a nice finishing technique.

keep moving. If he delivers a roundhouse kick, trap the leg with your arm and continue your entry. Even if you miss catching the leg, you have still closed the distance. And if you capture the leg, you can move in for a leg sweep and take him down.

When closing the gap to your opponent, hold your head high so you can see where you are going. This also allows you to penetrate your shoulder deeply into your opponent's body and to maintain control once you are in grappling range. Don't grab him with your arms until your body is against his. This ensures good penetration and a tight clinch. Once your body is tightly pressed to the opponent, lock your hands together around his body; allow him no room to move or strike you. "After the clinch, it doesn't matter what happens," Carlos Machado says. "One way or another, we're going to hit the ground, and we'll be in my world. The ground is my ocean, I'm the shark, and most people don't even know how to swim."

Takedowns

Once you have the opponent in a clinch, the only strikes he can land are elbow and knee smashes, and head butts. A good grappler eliminates the possibility of even these techniques by bringing his body in close and to the side of the opponent. Even if the clinch isn't perfect, your momentum is usually enough to quickly knock him off-balance, at which time his continued striking becomes ineffective or impossible.

If you are still standing after the clinch, you can use any of several basic takedowns. Always keep your body close to your opponent's so you can maximize your ability to use leverage against him and bring him to the ground.

Two common Brazilian-jujutsu takedowns are essentially judo techniques. The first is an inside leg wrap, achieved by putting your right leg between your opponent's legs and wrapping your right leg heel first around his left leg. Force his weight past his left leg, which will trip him and take both of you to the ground. The weight of your body should be borne by him; his body acts as a cushion for you when you hit the ground.

"It is very difficult to maintain your balance in a tense and fast-moving situation," Jean Jacques Machado says. "Add to that a second body attached to your own, and gravity is going to have the last word."

The second takedown is an outside leg wrap, in which you place your right leg outside of your opponent's legs, then wrap it around his left leg. Use your right heel to scoop his left foot as you spin your body and his to the right. Because he no longer has his left foot for support, you both go

Brazilian-jujutsu stylists often use a knee-stomping technique (1) to close the fighting distance on their opponent and open (2) a pathway to a clinch.

down. Once again, his body acts as your cushion.

A third basic takedown is the "spine squeeze," a wrestling move in which you lock your arms around your opponent's lower back. With your right leg forward, pull tightly and bring his hips and lower back toward you while driving your right shoulder high into his body. This forces him off-balance and to the ground. Release your grip as you fall so your hands do not become trapped under his body.

Two other popular takedowns are called "duck-unders." They are executed by ducking under your opponent's arm and moving to a safe position beside or behind him. As you move around his body, duck your head under his arm and keep your body tight against his. Once you move to his side or back, you are ready to take him down. From this position, you may decide to use a foot sweep. Bring the opponent to your right side and begin to lift him off the ground. Use the bottom of your left foot to sweep his left foot into his right foot. This swings him first onto his side, then sideways to the ground. You can lower your weight onto him without taking a fall yourself.

You can also use a duck-under technique and finish in a sitting position. This is popular because you wind up on top of your opponent in a mounted position. After completing the duck-under maneuver and moving behind the opponent, keep your arms wrapped tightly around his waist like a seat belt.

A palm strike (1) to the opponent's face can allow the Brazilian-jujutsu stylist to close the fighting distance and grab (2) the backs of his adversary's knees. He can then lift (3) his opponent and dump him (4) on his back. A painful foot lock (5) is an effective submission follow-up technique.

Twist to your left and sit on the ground with your right leg bent and your left leg extended. This trips the opponent backward, and his momentum allows you to swing your body around and land on top of him. His struggle to remain standing makes your drop to the ground very soft.

Another favorite Brazilian-jujutsu takedown is the double-leg attack. Rather than beginning from a bear hug, this takedown relies on clasping your hands around the outside of your opponent's knees. Because you run the risk of being struck in the face, Rigan Machado suggests striking your opponent's face as you enter grappling range. This keeps him on the defensive, unable to react to your entry. "I like to fake to the face, then go for the legs," he says. "When you go for the clinch, always concentrate on hugging your opponent, never on what strikes are coming at you. You must move in with confidence."

To complete the move, bring your shoulder snug against the opponent's waist and clasp the outside of his knees. You can then lower your hips and lift him into the air. Once he is lifted, twist his body to the side and drop him to the ground. Or after grabbing his knees, thrust your shoulder forward and drive him back. Simultaneously pull his legs toward you, forcing him to fall on his back. Your finishing position allows you to control his legs.

Mixed Attacks

The Machados also advise students to acquire competence with one or two long-range fighting moves. Being able to throw a credible kick or punch keeps your opponent guessing about where the real danger lies. Best for grapplers are those strikes—such as the previously mentioned knee stomp—that allow them to immediately follow up into a clinch.

No matter which takedown technique you use, never second-guess yourself. Once you begin your entry, follow through 100 percent. A strong will and steady momentum will help ensure a safe clinch and takedown. The last thing you want is to give a good puncher or kicker a second chance to hit you. If you move in and get stunned by a blow, hang on to the opponent until you recover and can continue. You can practice takedowns with partners who have control, allowing them to try to hit you. In this way, you become accustomed to being hit and overcome the fear of contact.

SHOOTFIGHTING
Brutally Effective Moves Promise a Submission From Any Position

by Lowell P. Thomas • February 2000

We've been sparring for a couple minutes, just feeling each other out. This guy is one tough dude, so I'm really careful. I put a palm strike into his forehead and follow it with a *muay Thai* kick to the inside of his left thigh. I figure he's ready now. Instead of the kick, I follow my next strike with a step behind, a grab around the waist and a takedown over my hip. Forcing his arm to the right, I shoot my left arm around his neck and lock it onto my right arm for a sleeper hold. If I apply too much pressure, he may pass out. I'm not too concerned with this guy, however, because he knows what he's doing. He elbows his left arm past my head, locks his hands around my waist and flips me over his chest and onto my back. Now I have to move quickly or he will catch me with a side-body head lock. I apply pressure, aiming to dislocate his shoulder.

Less than a second later, I've lost the whole shooting match. All my opponent did was somersault out of the chicken wing, drop his knee onto my face and armbar my left arm against his head. That series of movements freed up his right hand to punch me in the ribs.

A lot of stupid things flash through my mind. For example, I wonder whether the sequence is related to *aikido* immobilization technique No. 2 or No. 3. I am feeling pain, gasping for breath and at a loss for an escape. My opponent's next move surprises me: Instead of destroying my left arm and breaking my ribs, he just chuckles and lets me go. "OK," he says. "Now I'll take you down and you can escape."

Fundamental Strategies

That sequence was a shootfighting technique meant to demonstrate what the art is all about. Barry Polonitza, the tough dude who could have really hurt me, is a senior shootfighting instructor in Bart Vale's International Shootfighting Association. As Polonitza guided me through my moves, the contact stayed light; all chokes and locks were released as soon as I tapped. Still, I was impressed. From a stand-up kick-and-punch strategy, Polonitza had me slide into a takedown with a fake kick, then move to a choke. From there, we worked on defensive and offensive counters.

I have never claimed to be the quickest learner in the world, but I was able to apply a sequence of basic shootfighting locks, chokes and counters

Photos by Eric Dusenbery

To illustrate shootfighting's versatility, Bart Vale (left) executes a midlevel roundhouse kick, which is trapped by his opponent (1). Vale immediately dives for the opponent's left leg (2). Once he falls to the mat, Vale executes a foot lock (3).

after one hour of practice. Obviously, the rate at which a martial artist attains real skill depends on several factors: the amount of instruction, the initial level of skill he possesses and his willingness to work hard.

The fundamentals of shootfighting are easy to learn. Beginners use powerful, effective techniques in the first few hours of training. It is a logical art in that it uses each new move to build the previous one. First comes the basic fighting stance. The jab comes next, and that leads to the cross and the muay Thai kick to the inner and outer thigh. To counter those kicks, you learn the appropriate leg blocks.

The next series of shootfighting techniques includes a fake kick, a grab around the waist, a takedown and a sleeper choke. At this stage, things

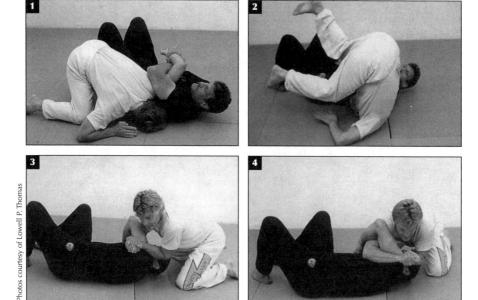

The strength of shootfighting lies in its flow drills. To demonstrate, Vale locks Barry Polonitza's left arm in a "chicken wing" (1). Because Vale neglected to trap his opponent's leg to prevent him from escaping, the other man is able to somersault out of the hold (2). From his new position on top (3), the opponent can begin attacking Vale's left arm and shoulder (4).

start getting serious if you're a karate practitioner. By the time you are lying on your side with a sweaty forearm driving into your carotid artery, you will have figured out that it's too late to use the standard side kick. You've got only a couple seconds to do the right thing. What you need is a technique that can break the choke hold and let you roll your opponent into a side-body head lock that will take his breath away.

The method of teaching shootfighting requires you to run through these chains of offensive and defensive moves. The next time your favorite offense is countered and you find yourself locked under some big gorilla, you can apply the next option.

You need approximately two hours to grasp the basic movements I mentioned above. Shootfighting seems to stick in your head. There's something about close contact with another human body that gets imprinted on your brain. It took me weeks to learn a single karate *kata* (form), and it was years after that before I began to really understand how to execute it. The best thing about shootfighting is that it can be learned quickly.

Simple yet brutally effective, it is a progressive stand-alone self-defense system that begins with kicking and punching, progresses through knee and elbow strikes, and advances to takedowns, chokes and joint locks. If you've already mastered a stand-up art such as karate or *taekwondo,* shootfighting will enable you to finish things once you are on the ground. When I say "finish," I mean it: These are not "pretend" movements but serious submission techniques that must be used carefully in and out of the *dojo* (training hall).

Amateurs and Professionals

Watching professional bouts is the best way to comprehend the effectiveness and versatility of shootfighting. The fight-ending possibilities available to a pro are astonishing because they work from virtually any position and with virtually any technique. I have seen matches completed after a throw, a kick to the leg, a palm-heel strike to the head, as well as numerous chokes and joint locks. Professionals are allowed to employ a fuller range of techniques than amateurs, and their matches have no time limit. Amateur matches are limited to 15 minutes. Both professionals and amateurs use arsenals of strikes, throws, locks and chokes designed to force their opponent to concede. If a shootfighter applies a lock on you, you feel his entire body weight moving into that lock. You have no option but to tap or counter with an escape. To resist is to court agonizing pain and potential injury. The techniques that are most likely to seriously injure a fighter—such as a groin strike or fist to the face—are restricted in amateur and professional fighting. However, on the street anything goes.

Submission techniques can be real eye-openers because most Western martial artists do not study a serious combat system, or what the Japanese called *bujutsu.* Instead, they study a form of *budo* (martial way), such as *karate-do,* aikido, *hapkido,* taekwondo or judo. These structured, idealistic ways are taught to large groups of adults and children without exposing them to danger. They teach fine stand-up skills, self-confidence, fitness, cooperation and spirituality, but unfortunately they often lack effective ground-fighting and finishing techniques. And those are the skills you need after your opponent takes you down and starts fighting tooth and nail to mess you up. I can say that because my background is in karate. I respect the legendary founders and the tradition their art instills, but when it comes to serious ground fighting, I have no doubt that karate did not teach me the skills I need to get myself out of danger.

History

More than two decades ago, two expert Japanese martial artists named Masami Soranaka and Toshiaki Fujiwara recognized the deficits in the traditional martial ways. With the aid of Karl Gotch—who is considered by many to be the best serious wrestler of all time—they supplemented their own martial arts with takedown techniques and submission grappling. By combining those moves with a hefty dose of muay Thai kickboxing, they synthesized shootfighting, an art that possesses the effectiveness of a .44-caliber handgun. In Japan, shootfighting—also called "strong-style fighting," or *kyo sho kai*—has become the third most popular spectator sport, falling behind baseball and sumo.

Although professional shootfighting got off to a slow start in Japan, it is now extremely popular there. Because audiences were familiar with only the fights of huge sumo wrestlers, battles between the lighter, more mobile shootfighters seemed strange. One reason why shootfighting may have taken awhile to catch on is that some spectators thought the bouts were phony—mere rehearsed performances like those in professional wrestling. They were wrong.

To boost the popularity of his art, Soranaka traveled to the United States in 1984 to recruit some strong, talented Americans. At a martial arts demonstration in Miami, he found a prime chunk of fighting meat: Bart Vale. Vale weighed 250 pounds and stood 6 feet 4 inches tall, yet he was very quick. Soranaka had never seen an American fighter of that size who could kick and move as wonderfully as Vale. Once the demonstration ended, Soranaka cornered his quarry, and in broken English, he asked Vale whether he wanted to travel to Japan to become a shootfighter.

Initially, Vale thought Soranaka was joking. When Soranaka realized he was not being taken seriously, he repeated his message: "You come Japan, I pay, you train."

The wheels turned in Vale's head: a trip to Japan, money and a chance to show off his skills. It might be fun, he thought, so he said, "OK ... maybe. What's shootfighting like?"

Soranaka just smiled and spoke a few more words: "OK, like kickboxing. OK, you fight, I pay."

To check out the offer he had just received, Vale traveled to Tampa, Florida, with Soranaka. Upon entering the gym, Vale was introduced to a young Japanese shootfighter with a tough mug. He sized up the guy and thought: "This dude weighs only about 180 pounds! Is this a joke?"

Nobody there spoke much English, so when he asked about the rules,

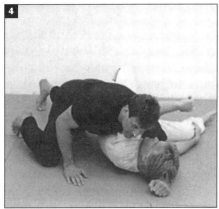

Vale assumes a fighting stance as he faces Polonitza (1). Vale blocks his opponent's punch and attacks the inside of his left thigh with a Thai kick (2). Vale then fakes a kick to create an opening so he can step past the opponent's left leg and slip his left arm around the other man's body for a takedown (3). Once on the ground, Vale wraps his left arm around the opponent's neck (4) and applies a choke that constricts the carotid artery (5).

he received the usual response: "OK, like kickboxing. You fight, OK?"

The match ended as quickly as it began. The Japanese fighter caught Vale's first kick and calmly transformed it into an ankle lock that took the American down, injuring his knee. Lying on the floor, Vale yelled: "Hey, you're cheating! Stop! Kickboxers don't grab kicks and twist knees!"

Soranaka laughed while he explained: "Not kickboxing, only like kickboxing. You go Japan. I pay."

Now Vale understood how shootfighting differed from kickboxing. He figured out that it was a little like kickboxing but encompassed much more: grabbing, taking down, locking, choking and submission from any position. It took that moment of pain and defeat for him to realize that he would have to learn shootfighting to round out his formidable sixth-degree black-belt Chinese-*kenpo* skills. He also vowed to train until he could jerk that young dude inside out.

Two weeks later, Vale followed Soranaka to Japan. With the exception of two brief visits back to the States, he trained there for four years straight. By 1988 he had acquired enough skill to work his way through the best of the professional shootfighters, including his own instructor, Yoshio Fujiwara.

Vale became a world champion and sports hero in Japan, where kids still collect trading cards that feature his image. Although he is not as famous in the States, he successfully runs his own organization, the Bart Vale International Shootfighting Association, which is based in Miami and has branches around the world. He is currently developing a stable of senior instructors to teach workshops and sponsor amateur exhibitions.

Recently, the organizers of the Olympics have begun paying attention to the future of shootfighting. The art can be assimilated into modern *pankration*, which is a revival of a Greek style of combat that is scheduled to make its debut at the 2004 Olympic Games in Athens, Greece. Not surprisingly, Vale has become a certified pankration coach. In that capacity, he will train fighters and conduct tournaments and workshops to prepare America's fighting representatives.

All Are Welcome

Although professional bouts are rough, beginners seeking self-defense skills or aspiring to amateur status can readily find a place in shootfighting to suit their needs and level of commitment. Women train alongside men, and children as young as 6 learn basic techniques.

In spite of its Japanese origins, it is a remarkably westernized art. There are no secrets. It is an in-your-face-right-here-right-now system of combat. The techniques taught during the first week of class are the same ones professional fighters use. Students train in sweat pants and a T-shirt to prevent them from depending on using the clothing as an aid.

Instead of belt rankings, the levels of attainment are signified by the color of the student's sweat pants. Beginners wear gray sweats through the first five levels, intermediate students wear red as they progress through the next three levels, and advanced students wear black while they work through the final five levels. Formalities are minimal, and there is no rigid stance, shouted instructions or one-punch-one-kill ideology. Instead, the emphasis is on correct form and the flow of attack and defense.

Becoming a shootfighting instructor requires about two and a half years of intensive training. Progression through the three instructor levels takes several additional years. Consequently, instructors are supremely capable of teaching any student—no matter which art he or she has studied—the punches, kicks, takedowns, joint locks, chokes, escapes and reversals needed to become a complete martial artist. If it worked for me, it can work for anyone.

10 KEYS TO GROUND SUPERIORITY
No Matter Which Style of Grappling You Practice, These Tips Will Make You a Better Fighter

by Matt Furey • Photos courtesy of Matt Furey • June 2000

Success leaves clues. That's something I've learned in my lifelong study of grappling. Whenever you see someone succeeding in a grappling art, you can study what that person has done, put the same keys to work in your own life and watch your actions bear fruit.

I have been blessed with teachers who have stood at the top of the grappling world. Their advice helped me become a national and world champion. No doubt, the techniques those men taught me were invaluable, but of even greater importance was their wisdom. The 10 keys to ground superiority listed below are a small part of what I learned, but they are some of the guiding principles of my life. If you follow them, you will find that they can be immensely helpful in your practice and your life. If you are not a grappler, don't despair; they apply to every martial artist.

Get in Condition

Catch-as-catch-can wrestling's foremost authority, Karl Gotch, is famous for his many witty sayings. One of them, though, is nothing but pure wisdom: "Conditioning is your best submission hold." There is no question that superior technique is important on the mat, but technique that lacks a solid foundation will eventually crumble. Moves you can do with ease when you're fresh become sloppy and ineffective when you're fatigued. Once fatigue sets in, your mind becomes weak and you become easy prey for an opponent who may not even be as technically advanced as you are.

Vince Lombardi, the legendary coach of the Green Bay Packers, once said, "Fatigue makes cowards of us all." He was right. Think about the

Get in condition: Matt Furey performs a Hindu push-up (1-2) to stretch and strengthen his upper body.

times in which you were filled with courage and confidence when a match began, then try to remember how quickly that courage evaporated when you realized that going the distance required more gas than you had in your tank.

When it comes to conditioning, Gotch identifies five areas that grapplers need to develop: strength, endurance, speed, agility and reflex. All five complement each other. If you have no endurance, you will find little use for your strength. Knowledge of specific techniques is nothing without the speed needed to execute them. Good reflexes tell you when to make your move, and agility helps you move in and out of position with ease.

Train Your Left Side First

Years ago when I began studying kung fu, I was struck by the fact that the instructor always had us learn our movements using our left side first. Most people, when left to their own devices, will practice new techniques on their favorite side—usually their right. Once they get better at a technique using their right side, they spend little or no time working the same technique on their left. They stay where they're comfortable. Trouble is,

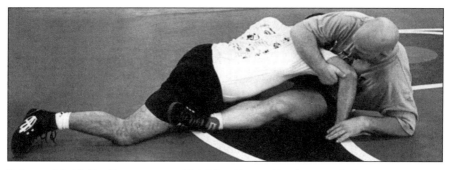

Train your left side first: Furey maneuvers his left hand into position for an arm lock.

most grapplers are most comfortable countering you on the same side you're working your offense from.

When a right-handed boxer begins to learn his art, what punch does he learn first? The left jab. There is something to be gleaned from that. If you begin learning on your left side, you're teaching the side of your body that has never been educated in the wrong method. More often than not, your right side knows how to move; the problem is that the movement on that side is stiff and improperly trained.

When you learn a technique on your left side first, you'll find it easier to train your right side to do the same movement later. The reverse is not true. Those who learn on their right side first have more trouble switching to their left—if they even try.

Don't limit yourself. Think how much more effective you will be when you can attack your opponent using either side of your body.

Wrestle With Shadows

Boxers I have spoken with estimate that 80 percent to 90 percent of their success is related to the amount of time they spend doing shadow work. On the Eastern side of the fence, karate and kung fu are well-known for teaching *kata* (forms), but these days many people frown on kata, claiming that they do not accurately represent "real fighting."

In reality, no method of training accurately represents real fighting—other than getting in real fights. You don't practice stretches during a fight. You don't hit bags or kick shields. You don't run sprints or lift weights. And you don't do push-ups on your knuckles. If those things aren't what you do in a real fight, why should you do them in practice? Why not toss everything aside and just go out and fight? That's all you really need, isn't it?

There are many benefits to shadowboxing and kata practice. They develop mental focus, timing and athleticism. With regard to grappling, I suggest that students "wrestle with shadows." You cannot always count on having a training partner, and even when you do, you get a psychological benefit from shadow work that you cannot get from sparring.

Olympic champion wrestlers Dan Gable and John Smith swore that shadow wrestling was essential to their success. They practiced the same type of skill that all boxers take for granted. Do what the great ones have done, and you'll know why they recommend it.

Expect the Unexpected

Never train for a match thinking that you know everything your opponent will do. On one hand, you'll want to prepare a strategy that will defeat your opponent's best weapons. On the other hand, there will be times when you come up against someone you know nothing about. If you have done your best to work from every angle and have covered every possibility you can think of, you'll be better off technically and you'll go into an encounter with greater confidence.

The element of surprise is something you should always bear in mind when you train. When an opponent catches you in a hold you didn't expect, one thing is certain: Escaping from it is difficult. And even if you do get

Expect the unexpected: The opponent attempts to finish Furey with a heel hook (1), but Furey surprises him by repositioning his body (2) and shoving the opponent's right leg across his body (3). Furey eventually escapes from the hold and controls the other man (4).

out, you'll be exhausted afterward. If, however, you have prepared for the worst, you'll have a much better idea of what to do.

Never assume that the worst will not happen to you. Begin your practice from the positions you don't want to be in. Maybe you're being held in a head lock. Maybe you're on your stomach fighting your way out of a stranglehold. If you lack confidence in those areas, you need to work on them. Expect that your opponent has the skills to put you in a punishing predicament and learn how to counter it. When you can do that, it'll be harder for anyone to surprise you.

Don't Go Fishing Without Bait

Many grapplers attempt takedowns and submissions without setting them up first. That way of fighting may work against beginners, but if you want to fish with those who are beyond the novice stage, you'll need some bait. In fact, it is a good idea to have several types of bait—unless, of course, you're interested in catching only one type of fish.

Setups are part of each takedown, throw and submission. Having a variety of setups in your arsenal is like having a tackle box filled with lures. You might be able to catch one type of fish with one type of lure, but if you want to be lord of the fish, you'll need to use a different lure and quite possibly a different strategy for each type of fish you're attempting to land.

The same holds true for grappling. Know your opponent and study him well, then sucker him into the moves you want to beat him with.

Keep Rocking the Boat

Imagine that you are in the middle of a quiet lake in a small boat. You're lying in the sun and trying to relax, but every few seconds, someone in another boat nudges you. Each time it happens, you fear your boat will tip over. You stand up and try to persuade the other guy to stop, but he persists. Now you're having trouble keeping your balance. You're helpless against the aggressor, and eventually you lose your footing and fall into the water.

Now if the aggressor bumped into your boat only one time, chances are that little if anything would happen. Sure you'd be irritated, but you

Keep rocking the boat: If you continuously execute moves your opponent does not expect, you will keep him off-guard and make it difficult for him to attack. To illustrate, Furey pushes his opponent's shoulder (1) and shoves his arm downward (2). Furey then maneuvers the opponent's head using his right hand (3) and his left (4).

would not have lost your bearings. But each time he hits you, he does so from a different angle and direction. Before long, all you know is that you will get hit again, but where and how is a mystery. That alone will keep you off-balance and drain your energy.

That's what you should do to your opponent on the mat. Never give him a chance to relax. Keep him unsettled and uptight with movements that upset his balance. An opponent who is constantly trying to adjust his balance gets tired much more quickly than one who is left alone.

Train in a Variety of Outfits

Many martial artists train in only a *gi* (uniform). Others disdain the gi because people don't wear them when they fight in public.

Although no one wears a gi on the street, most areas of the world have four seasons and winter happens to be one of them. If you try to throw someone who is holding your jacket, you'll be surprised at how much harder it is. Never think that learning how to manipulate someone else's

Train in a variety of outfits: Furey, who is a national champion wrestler, also grapples in a shuai chiao kung fu uniform to prepare for competitions in which he must wear a prescribed outfit.

clothing is a waste of time.

Knowing how to attack and defend with and without traditional attire is important. Some of the movements you learn in grappling are strictly for sport, while others are for self-defense. But life is full of surprises, and you never know when you may need to modify your sport to protect yourself or your loved ones. That's why it is important to know the self-defense aspects of your art.

Training in different outfits is great for breaking up the monotony of practice. It also makes you a well-rounded martial artist who can make the most effective choices in a variety of situations.

Train Harder Than the Rest

Almost without exception, the people who excel in any field are the ones who train harder than everyone else. Genetics, natural ability and the like can take you only so far. The rest is up to you—and it's called "hard work."

Whenever you read about someone who has excelled in your art, find out how he trained. What exercises did he do? How often did he do them? How many hours did he spend working out each day? How long has he followed that regimen?

When you have the answers to those questions, one thing will be evident: People who are at the top didn't just land there. Luck, genetics and biorhythms are not the keys to success. Luck is what happens when you have prepared yourself thoroughly and have a single-minded focus on an objective. Train hard and concentrate on achieving worthwhile goals, and you will move up the ladder of success.

Ask Yourself Why

I once heard a story about a large family that gets together for its annual reunion. A young bride is seen cutting off the end of the ham before she puts it into the oven. A curious onlooker asks why. The lady says that her mother

Ask yourself why: Grappling instructors frequently tell their students to avoid using their thumb while performing certain techniques (left), but most do not know why that is any better or worse than using the thumb (right).

taught her. The onlooker then asks the mother the same question. "I don't know why we do that," she says. "That's what my mother taught me."

The grandmother is also at the reunion, so the onlooker tracks her down as well and asks her the same question. "I don't know why they do it," the grandmother says. "But when I grew up, I cut off the end because our pan was too small."

How many times have you asked your teacher to explain why you do a move a certain way? Chances are that the answer had something to do with tradition. That explanation is no better than the one given for cutting off the end of the ham.

The same point applies to grappling. You may be following orders regarding the mechanics of executing a certain hold, but there is a chance that the traditional method you've been taught is not the most effective way. Perhaps you are cutting off part of your body—figuratively speaking, of course—and doing so hinders your performance.

I have spoken to many grapplers who were taught to never use their thumb while executing various submission holds. When I ask them why they don't use their thumb, they say: "I don't know. All I know is that my teacher said never use it." When I ask them if not using their thumb makes any sense, most admit that it does not.

The next time you are told not to use your thumb (or any other body part) while executing a hold, you should ask why. If the answer sounds a bit like cutting off the end of the ham, search for a better explanation.

Think

In the gyms where Gotch used to train Japanese wrestlers, he posted the word "think" on each wall because he believed it was the most important lesson he could teach them. He also believed it was the most neglected skill of students of combat.

Henry Ford once said, "Thinking is the hardest work on earth—that's why so few people engage in it." The grappler who engages in the "hardest work on earth" immediately puts himself ahead of most others in the field.

When you practice, don't simply be someone who wants everything handed to him on a silver platter. Think. Use your brain. Ask yourself questions. Put yourself in positions and figure out what you can do to counter each hold. Think of different setups for your holds. Experiment. Try new things.

After practice, continue to think about what you can do to make yourself better. The more time you spend thinking about the grappler you want to become, the faster you will achieve your goal.

ATTACKS AND TRAPS FROM THE GUARD
5 Winning Brazilian-Jujutsu Techniques From Pedro Sauer

by Ella Morse • December 2001

Combat has been part of Pedro Sauer's life since he was 5. That's the tender age at which he took up the sweet science of boxing. Later he added *taekwondo* and judo to his résumé, but it was not until he had turned 15 that the Rio de Janeiro, Brazil, native experienced an epiphany: Childhood chum Rickson Gracie introduced him to his dad, Helio Gracie.

"Oh, you're a boxer," the revered founder of Gracie *jujutsu* said to the boy. "Let me see how you do." The Gracie patriarch then had Sauer spar with his 8-year-old son, Royler Gracie. As the teenager expended his final ounces of energy fighting off Royler Gracie's choke, he saw the light. Recognizing the effectiveness of the grappling art, Sauer returned to the school the next day and signed up.

A self-described fanatic for the Brazilian interpretation of the Japanese art, Sauer trained seven days a week. Helio Gracie took him under his wing, and for six years, he supplemented his expanding knowledge base with private lessons from Rickson Gracie. "He was the guy who showed me everything I know," Sauer says.

After graduating from college, Sauer put in 11 years as a stockbroker in Brazil, but he eventually realized his interests lay in mutual combat, not mutual funds. He then decided to move to the United States to pursue his dream of teaching jujutsu. When he relocated to California in 1990, the man who helped him obtain a green card was none other than Chuck Norris, whom Sauer had met in Brazil in 1985. Once he settled in, he lived with Rickson Gracie and trained extensively with his father, brothers and cousins.

In December 1990, Sauer moved to Utah and introduced the South American art there. He rapidly built a reputation as one of the best instructors in the United States. The 43-year-old has enjoyed such success for several reasons: He holds a fifth-degree black belt from the Federacao de Jiu-Jitsu and a third-degree from Rorion Gracie. In fact, he is the first person outside the Gracie family to earn a black belt and teach in the United States. Sauer is now striving to build up his own school, the Pedro Sauer Brazilian Jiu-Jitsu Academy in Salt Lake City. More than 2,000 students there and in 20 affiliate schools across the United States are developing under his guidance, and even more experience his wisdom in the weekly seminars he conducts across the country. In addition, he teaches elite protection units such as SWAT teams, the FBI and the CIA.

"Now I'm trying to go a little bit away from Brazilian jujutsu and build Sauer jujutsu," he says. One thing he hopes his new system will do is inculcate students with more respect, self-confidence and self-discipline as they learn the best grappling techniques and strategies in the world. The following are five of those gems.

Deceptive Attack

One of Sauer's favorite offensive strategies is a deceptive little number he calls the double attack. It is used to set up an opponent for an armbar. Start on your back with your opponent in your closed guard. Then dig your right hand in deep and grab the back of his collar. Next, extend your

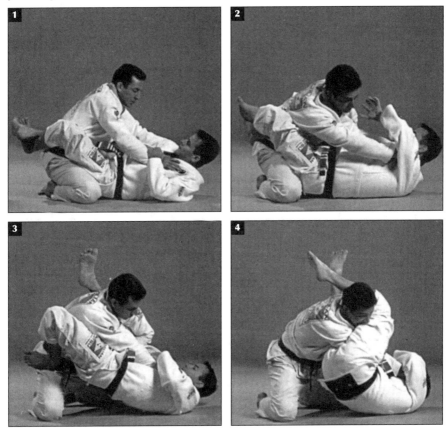

Deceptive attack: Pedro Sauer lies on his back with Frank Cucci in his guard (1). Sauer uses his right hand to hold the right side of his opponent's collar and his left hand to attempt to grab the other side to execute a choke (2). When the opponent tries to resist the choke, Sauer "climbs" his body with his legs (3) and executes an armbar (4).

left arm in front of his face to accomplish two goals: to prevent him from moving his arm and to make him think you will grab the other side of his collar to execute a choke.

When he tries to fight off the attempted choke, Sauer says, open your legs and "climb" up his body. That will prevent him from escaping while you trap his extended arm and swing your left leg over his head. The armbar is executed when you use your hips and back to hyperextend his arm. For added security, keep your lower legs flexed to limit his chances for escape.

Role Reversal

Sauer has a preferred method for reversing the mount quickly and efficiently, and it also involves a bit of subterfuge. Start with your opponent in your guard. Sink your right hand in and grab the right side of his collar, then insert your left hand and grasp the left side. If he does not detect the danger of the choke, go ahead and execute it. He'll tap in a few seconds.

However, a savvy opponent will sense the danger and straighten his back to escape. That's your cue to let go with your left hand and begin shifting your weight onto the left side of your body. Immediately wrap your right

Role reversal: Sauer holds Cucci in his guard and threatens him with a collar choke (1). When the opponent straightens his back to escape, Sauer releases his left hand and turns his body (2). The Brazilian-jujutsu expert then wraps his right arm around the opponent's right arm and slams his hips into him (3). The opponent is swept to the mat, and Sauer lands on top (4).

arm around his extended right arm, thrust your hips against his chest and rotate your trunk counterclockwise. He will be swept to the mat, and you will land on top of him. From that mounted position, any number of finishing techniques can be employed.

Opposites Attack

Brazilian jujutsu is all about options, Sauer says. If a technique is

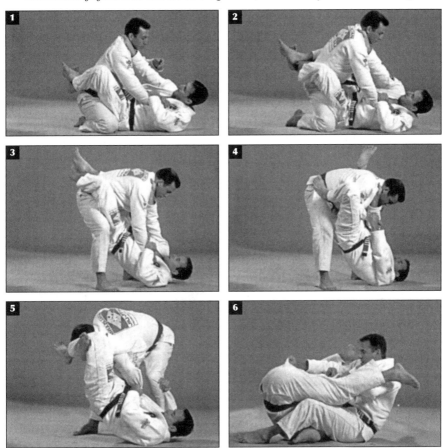

Opposites attack: Sauer holds his opponent in the guard and makes him think he will execute an armbar (1). The opponent scrambles to his feet so he can pass the guard (2-3). Sauer then releases his legs and places his left foot on the other man's right hip (4). Next, the Brazilian-jujutsu expert wraps his right leg around the opponent's left arm and locks that foot behind his left knee (5). To finish, Sauer rolls the opponent forward (6) and executes the armbar while immobilizing his left leg (7).

blocked, you must be ready to instantly transition into one that is just as effective. For example, set your opponent up for an armbar by holding him in your guard and using your right hand to grab the right side of his collar and your left arm to pin his right arm against your chest. Most likely, he will climb to his feet in an attempt to pass the guard. As he uses his arms to push downward on your stomach, maintain your hold on his right arm and collar.

Next, place your left foot on your opponent's right hip, turn your body sideways and focus your attention on the opposite side of his body, Sauer says. "Wrap your right leg around his left arm and lock your legs in a triangle around it."

Then grab his left leg with your right arm and, if he tries to step over your head, send him tumbling headfirst onto the mat. "He will roll and end up on his back in an armbar," Sauer says. If necessary, hold his left leg for extra control, he adds.

Clean Sweep

If you are holding your opponent in the closed guard, another way to deceive him starts with planting your hands on opposite sides of his collar for a possible choke and pulling his upper body in close. If he reacts

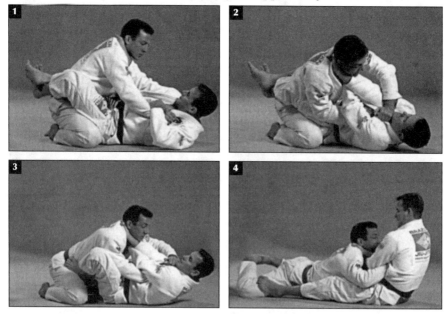

Clean sweep: With his opponent in the closed guard, Sauer once again prepares to execute a choke (1). The opponent responds by attempting a choke of his own (2). Sauer then plants his feet on the other man's hips (3) and sweeps his base out from under him, leaving him unable to resist (4).

by attempting a lapel choke of his own, place your heels on his hips and straighten your legs to sweep his base out from under him. He will wind up flat on his stomach, unable to defend against your frontal choke.

Changing Targets

Sauer's final bit of jujutsu trickery also starts with you on your back and your opponent in your guard. If he inserts his left arm between your right leg and his own ribs in an attempt to pass the guard, use your right hand to grab the right side of his collar and your left hand to control his right arm. As soon as he maneuvers his left arm under your right thigh and grabs your lapel, bend your right leg around his neck and lock on a triangle choke.

If your opponent is well-schooled in Brazilian jujutsu, he will probably

Changing targets: Sauer lies on his back, and Cucci tries to pass the guard (1). Sauer begins to apply a triangle choke (2), and the opponent stands to escape (3). As soon as the opponent has relieved the pressure of the choke (4), Sauer switches gears and uses the triangle lock to hyperextend his arm (5).

straighten his back and try to stand. That may eliminate the pressure on his neck, but you will still have control of his right arm. To finish him, simply reverse your triangle choke so that instead of tucking your right foot behind your left knee, you now tuck your left foot behind your right knee and apply pressure to his hyperextended arm. "It's basically the same triangle hold," Sauer says. "It's just being done on the arm."

Common Mistakes

One of the most frequent mistakes fighters make when they try to execute these five techniques is using too much power, Sauer says. "When you rely on your muscles, it's yours against his, so you will find a lot of resistance if he is stronger."

The trick is to focus on where your body is in relation to his so you can use your brain to overcome his strength, he says. "If you look for the correct body position, you have more leverage to accomplish your techniques."

If you are unfortunate enough to get caught in one of these locks during training, remember that the consequences can range from a bit of pain to a minor bruise to a dislocated joint, Sauer says. "You really can get hurt, so to stay safe, it's wise to tap before you even feel the pressure." That way, you will ensure that you're always in top condition to master the best Brazilian-jujutsu deception techniques for fighting from the guard.

BRAZILIAN-JUJUTSU PRIMER
The Half-Guard
by Robert W. Young • June 2002

To say that practitioners of Brazilian *jujutsu* have honed their grappling skills into a fine art is to state the obvious. Because of them, nearly everyone in the martial arts world—especially those who follow mixed-martial arts competition—now possesses at least a rudimentary understanding of the basic positions of ground fighting, including the guard, the mount and the side control.

Somewhat less well-known is the half-guard position. The fact that it does not manifest itself in competition quite as often as the "big three" positions does not in any way mean it's ineffective on the mat; rather, it means that once you learn how to fight offensively from that position, you will be able to take your unknowing opponent by surprise. As many experts advise their students, the best way to defeat an opponent is to beat him with what he doesn't know.

Expert Advice

To obtain the best possible instruction in the offensive use of the half-guard, *Black Belt* sought help from Roberto Correa de Lima, who is better known by his nickname "Gordo," which means "fat" in Portuguese. (He was reportedly a plump tyke.) Correa is a 31-year-old graduate of the Gracie Barra Academy in Brazil. He started training in 1985 under Carlos Gracie Jr. and received his black belt in 1993.

When Correa competed in Brazil, his trademark technique was the half-guard, which he employed not just defensively but also with maximum aggression. A twist of fate led him to develop that somewhat unusual game plan: He sustained a serious injury to his left knee and was not able to fight from the full-guard while it healed. But that proved to be merely an inconvenience, and once he had perfected his half-guard strategy and techniques, he rolled to victory in the World Jiu-Jitsu Championships in 1996 and 1997, the Pan-American Jiu-Jitsu Championships in 1995, 1996, 1997, 1998 and 2001, and the Brazilian National Jiu-Jitsu Championships in 1994, 1995 and 1998.

The following are four of Correa's favorite methods for fighting from the half-guard.

Half-Guard to Leg Lock

You and your opponent start in a kneeling position. Your right hand

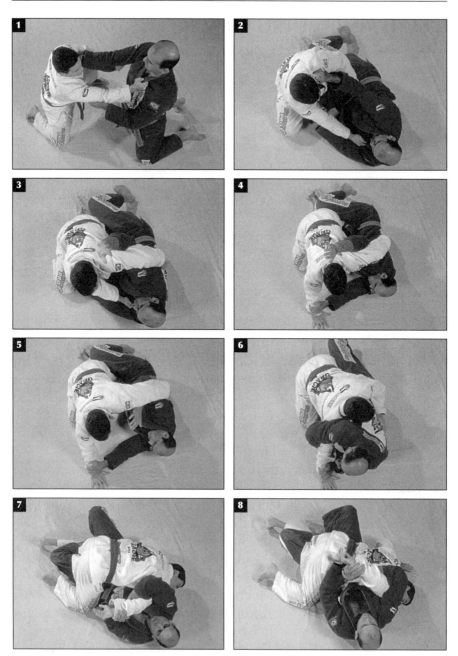

Half-guard to kimura: Roberto Correa de Lima (right) faces his opponent and holds his sleeve and lapel (1). He swings his legs forward to move into the half-guard, leaving his left leg wrapped around the other man's left leg (2). Correa then maneuvers his right arm under the opponent's left shoulder (3). As soon as the opponent plants his right arm on the mat, Correa grabs his wrist with his left hand (4). Next, the jujutsu expert repositions his right arm (5) and wraps it around his opponent's right arm while clamping his right hand onto his left forearm (6). As he lies backward (7), Correa executes the kimura (8).

holds his left lapel, and your left hand holds his right sleeve at the elbow. You then pull him forward as you fall onto your back and insert your left leg between his knees. After you bend your left leg so your shin lies across his left calf, place your right arm under his left arm to create more leverage. Next, shove his upper body to your left and sit up. After extracting your left arm from underneath his torso, use both hands to secure his left ankle. The leg lock is effected as you try to forcibly bend his leg while your left shin is wedged behind his knee.

Be forewarned that some Brazilian-jujutsu competitions, especially those held in the United States, prohibit this leg lock. Check the rules before you try it in a match, and always be prepared to release the pressure as soon as your opponent taps to lessen the chance of injury to his knee.

Half-Guard to Kimura

Begin on your knees facing your opponent. Your right hand grasps his left lapel, and your left hand holds his right sleeve. Your first move is to swing your legs forward and land on your back while simultaneously placing your left leg between his legs and pulling him into your half-guard. Next, "swim" your right arm under his left shoulder so you can generate the leverage you need to upset him. Then execute a feint to make him think you are trying to get to his back. As he reacts, grab his right wrist with your left hand. To finish, throw your right arm over his right humerus, then wrap your limb around his and lock your right hand onto your left forearm. As you lie back, apply pressure to his arm and shoulder using the *kimura* lock.

A skilled grappler will try to escape from this lock by rolling forward over your body. To prevent that, be sure to keep your left leg wrapped around his left leg as you crank his trapped arm behind his back.

Half-Guard Reversal

Once you have attained the half-guard position with your left leg placed on top of your opponent's left calf, position your right arm under his left arm. That enables you to create the leverage you need to open enough space to maneuver. Then grab the lower right portion of his uniform with your left hand and feed it to your right hand, which is reaching around his back. At the same time, your right knee moves into the open space that exists in front of his left hip. Once your knee passes his hip and your shin is pressed against his belt, pull his uniform with your right hand and lift his right knee with your left hand. Those forces work in concert to flip him over your

Half-guard reversal: The opponent begins in Correa's half-guard (1). Correa grabs the right side of his uniform with his left hand and feeds it around his back to his right hand (2). With his right shin positioned against the other man's hip (3), Correa pulls his uniform with his right hand and lifts his knee with his left hand (4). The opponent is flipped onto his back, and Correa lands in the side-control position (5).

body and deposit him on his back. You finish in the side-control position, from which you can effect a submission or transition to the mount.

Half-Guard Reversal to Mount

Starting on your back, place your left leg between your opponent's legs and drape your left shin across his calf to complete the half-guard. Your left hand grasps the lower right part of his uniform and pulls it toward his right hip, and your right arm extends under his left armpit and around his back. Then sit up and reach around his back with your right arm until you can grab the trapped portion of his uniform top. Once your left hand releases its grip on the uniform, it moves to control his right elbow. Next, place your right foot under his left leg to create leverage for a hook sweep. Finally, lean toward your left elbow, breaking his balance. Because you have trapped his right arm, he cannot use it to prevent himself from rolling onto his back. Ride him as he is swept, ending up in the mount position. From there, any number of submission holds are at your disposal.

Hitting the Mat

If you're trying to perfect your skills in Brazilian jujutsu, it is imperative to spend some serious time on the mat. Merely knowing how to fight

Half-guard reversal to mount: Correa starts on his back with Gerson Sanginitto in his half-guard (1). Correa's left hand holds the right side of the opponent's uniform and passes it to his right hand, which is reaching across his back (2). The jujutsu stylist then traps the opponent's right arm (3) and uses his right leg to execute a hook sweep and throw him onto his right shoulder (4). Correa stays face to face with his opponent as he rolls, winding up in the mount position (5).

from the half-guard will be of little benefit unless you have practiced your techniques until they become second nature. That training strategy helped Roberto Correa de Lima rise to the top of the Brazilian grappling world, and it can work just as well for you.

Jujutsu's Origins in South America

According to Rorion Gracie, Brazilian *jujutsu* can trace its origins to George Gracie's 1801 relocation from Scotland to Brazil. Years later, George's grandson, Gastão Gracie, befriended Esai Maeda, also known as Count Koma, the chief of a Japanese immigration colony who was assigned to Brazil in 1914. In gratitude, Maeda, a former jujutsu champion in Japan, taught his art to Carlos Gracie, Gastão's son. In 1925, Carlos and his four brothers opened the first jujutsu school in Brazil. Carlos' brother, Helio Gracie, later developed new techniques, smoothed out the transitions between them and crafted the undefeated system the family now teaches. "The essence is techniques that don't require strength, speed or coordination," Rorion said.

Royce Gracie, Rorion's brother, recounted a key episode involving his uncle, Carlos, and his father, Helio: "My dad was a small guy; he was very weak. So my dad would sit all day long just watching my uncle teach. One day, my uncle was late for a class, so my dad started teaching. From that day on, none of the students ever took a class with my uncle again. They liked my dad's new way."

Although the Gracie style of jujutsu derives its well-known effectiveness from Japanese jujutsu, its focus on ground fighting differentiates it from other brands of the ancient grappling art. "This style of jujutsu that we have, they are trying to hide so much in Japan—that's the story that I heard—that it became judo, *aikido* and the styles of jujutsu they have around here," Royce said. "They hid so much that they forgot their own art. The style we practice doesn't exist in Japan anymore."

—Editors

THE GROUND GAME
Pankration Still Rules After 3,000 Years!
by Nick Hines • Photos by C. Gardner and R.L. Jacques • December 2002

The term "mixed martial arts" refers to the modern concept of combining stand-up skills and ground fighting. Being a total fighter is now the rule rather than the exception. While integrating strikes, takedowns and submissions is a relatively novel idea to some, those who train in the Greek art of *pankration* know it's far from new. In fact, it dates back 3,000 years.

The ancient Hellenic combat sport has two components. *Ano* pankration is essentially the upright half. It uses punches, kicks, elbows and knees as striking tools, but it also includes takedowns, throws and chokes. *Kato* pankration refers to fighting on the ground and is the subject of this article.

Olympic Pankration of Antiquity

Classical pankration was essentially an all-out battle between two highly conditioned athletes. It featured bare-knuckle fisticuffs, kicking and submission wrestling. Only biting, gouging and stalling on the ground were prohibited. There were no time limits or weight divisions, and the participants, as was customary in Greek athletics, competed naked. Victory was declared when a beaten fighter could not continue or raised his index finger to submit.

Pankration differed from wrestling in that it permitted striking and kicking, and matches did not cease once a man was thrown or taken down. It employed an extensive set of striking techniques for standing combat, some of which were delivered with the open hand. The prevalent blow of this almost anything-goes contest was a lunging straight punch aimed at the head. While tight hooks and uppercuts were favored by Greek pugilists and those who engaged in ano pankration competitions, the strategy of kato pankration practitioners was to strike from a distance but grapple once inside. This is evidenced in classic artwork that depicts boxers going toe-to-toe while pankration stylists are shown lunging.

In the open style of pankration that was featured in the Olympics, much of the activity took place on the ground. Clinching occurred often, as did takedowns and throws. Once the fight went to the ground, the nature of the contest changed dramatically. Grappling became the focus of the action, with each man seeking the most advantageous position to control his opponent and execute his attack.

The ground arsenal included limb twisting, head locks and chokes. Striking also played a major role in the assault—which further differentiated pankration from another specialized method of grappling called *kato pale,* or ground wrestling. Evidence of the importance of striking while on

Passing the closed-scissors defense: Bryson Arvanitis holds Eric Hill by wrapping his legs around his waist (1). Hill attacks his opponent's eyes with his right hand (2), then steps out with his right foot while entangling his arm around the opponent's left leg (3). Hill maintains his grip on the leg as he pivots his body and steps over the opponent's torso (4). He then pins the leg to his chest (5) and leans backward into a kneebar (6).

the ground comes from two vase paintings: One depicts an athlete who is punching at his opponent's face to effect his release from a head lock, and the other shows a top-mounted fighter clutching his rival's throat while pummeling him with his free hand.

The hammerfist was an important striking weapon, especially when a fighter was mounted on his opponent's back. Scissoring the waist was also popular, especially when used with a rear strangle. History records how this very technique cost a two-time champion named Arrichion his life during the 54th Olympiad.

Although the rules against biting and gouging were strictly enforced, they were nonetheless broken, especially during heated ground conflicts. In fact, the militaristic Spartans, who did not compete in the Panhellenic games, encouraged those tactics in their local contests. One of Plutarch's narratives reminds us of the tough nature of their unique brand of pankration through an incident involving a man named Alkibiades, who had trained in Sparta. While competing in an Athenian gymnasium, he bit his opponent. The opponent became furious and screamed, "You bite just like a woman!" Alkibiades responded, "No! Just like a lion!"

The Rebirth

By 393, Olympic pankration had disappeared from the Hellenic sports scene. There is no documented evidence of Greece's legacy actively being practiced until its rebirth in 1969 by Greek-American Jim Arvanitis. He was the first to pioneer a modernized system that paralleled the achievement of his ancestors. This revolutionary style, called *mu tau*, served to update the original concepts with effective techniques for any combat situation.

Like most innovators, Arvanitis was ahead of his time. Because there was no such thing as pankration being practiced anywhere when he arrived on the scene, he took it upon himself to rebuild the sport from the ground up. One of the earliest proponents of cross-training, he studied those arts that he found most effective, carefully selecting the techniques that mirrored those used by the ancient Greeks. He credits combat judo and Greco-Roman wrestling as having the greatest influence on modern kato pankration.

Modern Practice

Arvanitis founded the United Pankration Alliance in 1984. Its mission was to standardize an educational blueprint for all those interested in representing the sport and to establish a set of rules that would encourage honor and spirited competition in the long tradition of the Hellenic culture. The UPA predates all other pankration groups, including the Hellenic Federation of Pankration Athlima based in Greece, which was formed in 1995. The following are the primary elements of contemporary sport pankration's ground game:

• **Transitioning to the Clinch:** Transitioning refers to closing the gap from long range to close-quarters grappling. It must be executed explosively and without hesitation to avoid receiving a shot to the head or face on the way in. When you move in low and focus your attack on your opponent's legs, the transition is called a "shoot." Transitions can be made as a direct offensive, as a follow-up to a strike or feint, or as a counter after a blow has been parried or evaded.

Once inside, clinch with your opponent, grasping him around the torso in preparation for a takedown. Although clinching the neck and tackling the legs are common, the Greeks are especially known for the waist lock,

Reversing the armbar: Hill has Brandon Arvanitis immobilized in a side armbar (1). Before the aggressor hyperextends the arm to effect a submission, Arvanitis bends his elbow and rolls to his right (2-3). He then slips out of the hold (4) and pounds his right fist into the opponent's ribs (5-6).

a type of clinch in which your fingers are interlocked and your arms are wrapped around the belt line. It can be used from the front or the back.

• **The Fall:** Once you secure the clinch, the ensuing technique is a hard takedown or throw, also known as the "fall." Among the most popular throwing skills are the shoulder throw and the suplex. Other methods include the foot sweep, which is especially effective after you have seized a kicking leg, and tripping, which is often executed by using a leg hook from the waist-lock position. Tackling the legs, popular in Greco-Roman wrestling, is also important in kato pankration. Single- and double-leg takedowns are excellent for scoring a fall—although your opponent, if he reacts quickly enough, can sprawl his weight on top of you or counter with a front guillotine choke.

• **Tactical Positioning:** Completing the fall, you will find yourself either on top of your adversary or under him. You must then neutralize and control his movements by obtaining a top- or side-mounted position from which a wide variety of attacks can be executed. If you are taken down, especially by the legs or waist, and are on the bottom, you should immediately go into a defensive posture by scissoring your opponent's waist with your legs in what has become known as the guard. As most grapplers know, this position offers many opportunities to submit a top-mounted aggressor. Whether you are employing an open guard (your feet are not crossed but are being used to hook your opponent's lower legs) or closed guard (your feet are locked at the ankles), your goal is to trap and immobilize him while going on the offensive.

• **Submission Tools:** Pankration teaches numerous techniques to force your foe to quit. Armbars, leg locks and chokes are effective whether you are attacking from the top or defending from the bottom. The use of strikes is also encouraged—not so much to knock the other combatant senseless but to weaken him and set up a finishing hold. In pankration's modern sport derivative, powerful body punches and knee blows are employed for this purpose. The ground-and-pound tactic seen in today's no-holds-barred events has long been a part of pankration.

The side armbar, hammer lock, key lock and inverted armbar are among the most effective arm-locking techniques. For the lower extremities, there are kneebars, heel hooks and toe holds. Particularly important in many of these techniques is the use of both legs to control one of the opponent's arms or legs. For example, in a side armbar or kneebar, you must learn to lock an elbow or knee between your thighs just above the crotch area to prevent an escape attempt.

Pankration chokes are applied with the arms or legs. They are designed to constrict the supply of blood or air through the carotid artery or windpipe, or to exert pressure on the Adam's apple to elicit a tap out. The three primary ground strangulation techniques in mu tau pankration are the rear choke, side choke and inverted leg choke from the guard.

• **Passes, Reversals and Rollouts:** These defensive maneuvers are designed to alter the control factor by enabling you to escape from a takedown, mount, guard or submission attempt. To make them work, timing is paramount. You must be aware of what your opponent is planning to do and keep one step ahead of him. You must also have a keen sense of where your weight is balanced and never rely on mere strength because doing so will sap your energy.

Contests Today

Modern pankration is not a precise duplication of its predecessor. In addition to not fighting in the nude, there are many regulations and safeguards to protect practitioners from injury. The following are guidelines established by the UPA:

• Open pankration is a contest that commences from the upright ready position following the "warrior salute" and can terminate either standing or on the ground.

• Legal stand-up techniques include punches to the head and body; kicks to the legs, body and head; knee thrusts to the head and body; clinching; throws; sweeps; takedowns; and submission holds.

• Legal ground techniques include punches, knee thrusts and kicks to the body; arm and leg submissions; and chokes.

• Among the illegal techniques are gouging; biting; groin strikes; head butts; hair pulling; elbowing; scratching; ear pulling; stomping on the feet, face or body; and fish-hooking.

• Victory is attained by knockout, technical knockout, default, submission or judge's decision. A KO is called if a competitor is knocked down by a punch, kick or knee thrust and cannot make it to his feet before a 10 count is finished. A TKO is called if the referee deems a fighter unfit to continue, if the second throws in the towel, or if a fighter is downed three times by a punch, kick or knee strike. A default is called when a fighter is disqualified or quits. A submission is called when a competitor taps out while standing or on the ground. A judge's decision will be rendered according to the accumulation of points based on various criteria.

• If a competitor is determined to be stalling on the ground, he and his opponent will be ordered to restart from a standing posture after 60 seconds.

History Repeats Itself

The 1990s have been described as the decade of mixed martial arts. Practitioners around the world now recognize the value of being multi-dimensional because fights often include a stand-up element and a ground element. By reading articles like this one, martial artists are rediscovering an art that has been inspired by the oldest of mixed-style combat in the world—one that teaches its students to punch, kick, throw and clinch while they are on their feet and to choke, lock joints and strike while they

Bottom-mount to top-mount switch: Brandon Arvanitis punches Hill from the top mount (1). Hill covers and pushes his opponent away with his left arm (2). He then rolls to his right while trapping the opponent's leg, thus preventing him from escaping (3). To finish, Hill gains the back-mount position (4) and strikes the other man's neck (5).

are on the ground.

Modern pankration is riding the wave of the MMA explosion—just as Arvanitis predicted 30 years ago. With its diverse technical skills, realistic approach to combat and specialized ground work, it is to today's athletes as it was to the Greek Olympians of old: the key to victory in any arena.

A kato pankration class at the Spartan Academy in Boston works on a shoulder lock.

JEET KUNE DO GRAPPLING, PART 1
When to Do It and When to Not Even Think About It

by William Holland • April 2003

Most people familiar with Bruce Lee have heard volumes spoken about his superhuman speed, amazing agility and spectacular street-fighting savvy. However, they are almost always surprised to discover that Lee invested a considerable amount of time in learning the grappling arts. If you need proof, flip to the Tools chapter of *Tao of Jeet Kune Do* and you'll notice numerous sketches of the "Little Dragon's" favorite throwing, choking and joint-locking moves. He knew that no matter how much a person might want to stay in punching or kicking range, a real fight can go to the pavement in a heartbeat. That's why grappling has always been part of the arsenal of a complete *jeet kune do* fighter.

Before Royce Gracie debuted in the Ultimate Fighting Championship, most skilled practitioners of pugilism—those who weren't into JKD—spent their time mastering hand and foot strikes. The fighters with a little more gumption spiced up their workouts with a dash of elbows and knees. Although many practiced judo and wrestling, they were just "grappling" and not really "fighting." But that was then and this is now. The rules have changed, and smart fighters in and out of the octagon have taken up cross-training in the striking and grappling arts. JKD practitioners and a few other nonconformists have always done it, but it's still a great time to re-examine Lee's take on ground combat.

 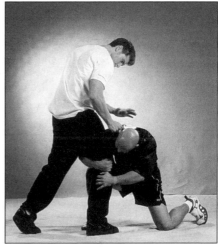

Jeet kune do instructors implore their students to never grapple against a knife. It's hazardous when you clinch (left) and when you shoot in for a takedown (right).

Ground Rules

Unlike judo, sport *jujutsu* and wrestling, JKD is meant for only one thing: the type of fighting that occurs on streets and in back alleys. As such, certain principles are emphasized when a JKD practitioner employs grappling in his overall blend of tactics and tools.

For one, the JKD fighter trains to be proficient in all ranges of combat: kicking, punching, infighting (also called trapping) and grappling. Being balanced in all four and trying to eliminate any weak links are the keys to becoming a skilled martial artist. Therefore, a JKD stylist can use grappling when he closes the distance, when the opponent closes the distance, when the opponent counters, after the opponent grabs his kick and so on. It's part of the flow.

Another key element of JKD is the need to maintain options while grappling. Although the student may be entangled in a ground position, he strives to maintain his ability to score a decisive punch, head butt, knee thrust or elbow smash while eliminating those attacks from the opponent's option list.

Although grappling may happen by design or default, the JKD stylist

Jeet kune do practitioners try to avoid locking up with multiple opponents because it is virtually impossible to control and finish more than one person at a time.

tries to maintain a superior position and the option of rising to his feet at any time to get mobile and strike back. Because he is always focused on reality in combat, he may opt to use grappling in one situation while avoiding it in another. He knows Sun Tzu's words of wisdom: The intelligent fighter brings his opponent to the field of battle and is not brought there by him. He takes his adversary to the ground when it suits his needs and avoids going to the ground when it might put him at risk. The following are some of the guidelines he strives to follow.

When Not to Grapple

Even though the JKD practitioner may not want to grapple in a given scenario, his opponent can take away his choice. Therefore, he learns how to take the war to the ground and trains until he can hold his own there. But if given a choice, he will resist becoming locked in a clinch or tumbling to the ground in certain situations:

• **Against an Opponent With a Blade:** Most instructors advise against closing the distance on or clinching with a knife-wielding enemy. Until the JKD fighter takes away or controls the weapon, he has no business getting in close. Of course, if the attacker charges in and leaves the defender no alternative, he will not hesitate to disarm or immobilize him, then throw him head over heels. In most other situations, however, the rule is to maintain distance and mobility, and seize any opportunity to blind him, break his kneecap or damage his weapon hand.

• **Against Multiple Opponents:** Whenever more than one attacker is present or possible, the ground is the last place the JKD practitioner wants to be. Even if he attains the much-vaunted mount position, he cannot protect himself from a swift kick in the ribs or knife in the kidney. The immediacy of this guideline was driven home for me when a friend who trains in Brazilian jujutsu and works as a police officer got in a fight while relaxing in a bar off-duty. His first instinct was to take the assailant to the floor, and he did. While he was jockeying for position to finish a lock, another hoodlum approached and kicked him numerous times in the back and head—all while the cop's backup gun was visible on his ankle.

• **When Mobility or Escape Is Essential:** If a situation has the potential to get ugly, the JKD student knows that a hasty exit is often the best response. Remember the Los Angeles riots and the more recent "celebrations" in which Lakers fans went wild after the team won? Fires were started, cars were trashed, stores were looted, and people were dragged from their vehicles and robbed. Obviously, these are battles best fought by others, but if a martial artist is forced to defend life and limb, he needs to stay on his feet and be able to retreat. Sometimes the smartest battles are the ones not fought.

• **Against a Superior Grappler:** If a JKD practitioner has a bigger, stronger, fiercer person in his face and that guy happens to be a more skilled ground fighter, he will attempt to force the assailant to fight a different game. The JKD stylist always strives to become skilled in kicking, punching, trapping and grappling ranges so that if grappling is not the key to victory on a given day, he can switch to another range—hopefully one in which he has the advantage over his opponent.

• **On a High-Risk Surface:** It doesn't take too much imagination to conceive of situations in which going to the ground can be hazardous to one's health. How about a construction site where nails, tools or sharp objects are lying about, or a back alley where broken bottles, used syringes and discarded auto parts litter the pavement? When a JKD practitioner stays on his feet, he improves his chances of avoiding all those nasty things.

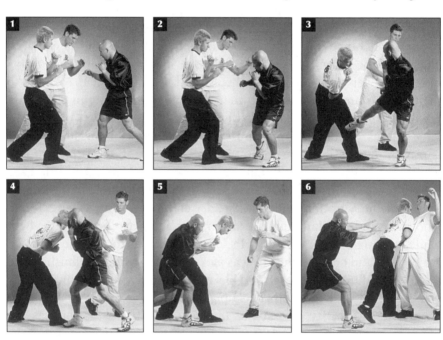

The preferred jeet kune do method for confronting multiple assailants involves rapid strikes and mobility. William Holland (right) faces two opponents (1). As the larger one punches, Holland angles slightly to his left to avoid the strike (2). The JKD stylist then plows a low stop-kick into the other man's lead knee using the "closest weapon, closest target" concept (3). He immediately yanks on the same man's neck to destroy his balance and prepares to maneuver around him (4). Next, Holland scoots behind the injured person and uses his body as a shield (5). Finally, he shoves the smaller assailant into the larger one to create enough distance and time to escape (6).

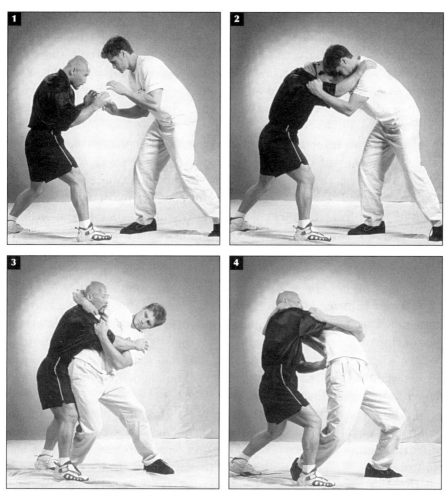

In jeet kune do, learning how to fight in all ranges means learning how to grapple as well as how to defend against grappling. Holland squares off with his opponent (1). The two men close the distance and tie up (2). The opponent positions his hips under Holland's center of gravity in preparation for a throw (3), but Holland counters the technique by shifting his body backward, pushing with his left arm and pulling with his right (4). With his balance ruined, the opponent has no choice but to fall backward.

When to Grapple

In addition to learning when not to grapple, the JKD student learns when going to the ground is the preferred course of action:

• **When Apprehending an Unarmed Assailant:** If the odds—relative skill, size, speed, mobility and so on—are stacked in his favor and the opponent has no weapon or cohorts, the humane thing for the JKD stylist to do is to take his opponent down and control him. That diminishes the need to shoot, stab or beat him into submission. From day one, police officers learn this strategy, which is covered in their use-of-force doctrine. They are taught to go from verbal commands to control techniques to pain-threshold moves to nonlethal weapons before resorting to deadly force or firearms. In instances when they have a less-than-cooperative person they must arrest, detain or otherwise control, grappling can help them accomplish the task and keep them out of court.

• **Against an Inferior Grappler:** When the JKD practitioner does not have to worry about bladed weapons, multiple assailants or dangerous ground, he can opt to shoot in, take down his opponent and maneuver him into his favorite submission hold. That approach is particularly valuable when he is confronted by a skilled striker because—whether you wish to admit it or not—a good grappler can outmaneuver and hogtie most stand-up fighters in a flash. And while most smart martial artists have figured out that a complete self-defense arsenal includes takedowns and grappling skills, many of them have yet to spend much time on the mat.

• **When Injuries Must Be Avoided:** This situation gets back to the humanitarian angle. The JKD fighter is taught to forget about the blood and guts of Hollywood movies and think about the litigious nature of American society. When Uncle Charlie has had one too many spiked punches at cousin Susie's wedding, the JKD stylist is better off taking a firm hold on his arm and escorting him to a more peaceful place.

• **When There Is No Alternative:** In the ring, in a back alley and in life, there are certain things that the martial artist has control over and other things that he doesn't. But no matter what happens, he always has control over how he deals with them. He may not be given a choice about whether to grapple, but he must deal with it. Once he acknowledges that combat on the ground is a possibility, he can train to prevail there.

The JKD Way

Jeet kune do grappling follows the same approach as JKD fighting in other ranges. It should be kept simple, direct and effective. The practitioner should strive for totality and a full utilization of his skills and strengths while minimizing his weaknesses. As opposed to memorizing dozens of techniques or forms, the JKD stylist who switches to grappling mode is more apt to focus on the feel and flow of his opponent and how his body, joints and limbs are positioned.

Remember that the JKD fighter is a finely tuned punching and kicking machine and will almost always strive to maintain a striking capacity—even when he's horizontal. The energy drills and sensitivity he has gained from sticky-hand drills and trapping exercises work well on the ground, and they can give him a sense of position, flow and opportunity that others seldom enjoy.

The jeet kune do fighter tries to be ready for anything during a fight. Here, Holland faces off against a grappler (1) and enters into a clinch (2). He then grabs the opponent's lead leg—or traps it if he tries to kick (3). Next, the JKD stylist executes a leg-sweep takedown, leaving the other man horizontal (4). Holland wraps his left arm around the trapped ankle for an Achilles lock, and to keep the assailant from squirming, he uses his right foot to pin his left thigh to the ground (5). The entire time, the JKD practitioner remains mobile and able to punch and kick.

JEET KUNE DO GRAPPLING, PART 2
Offensive Tactics for the Ground

by William Holland • May 2003

*P*art one of this series focused on the why's and when's of body-on-the-asphalt pugilism. Part two delves into its how-to component using the concepts of jeet kune do and presents the reader with a series of concise tips on training and fighting.

—W.H.

- A *jeet kune do* fighter strives to be proficient at all ranges of combat in all scenarios. He knows that against an aggressive fighter, he may need to use an intercepting fist, a stop-kick or a grappling technique.

- A grappling exchange can begin after the JKD stylist takes his opponent down, after he is taken down by his opponent or after one or both parties fall.

- One of the best ways for the JKD fighter to grapple with his adversary is to first convince him that grappling is the last thing on his agenda. If he wants to shoot in for a single- or double-leg takedown, he should fake a jab or cross to his opponent's head. As the opponent defends high, he will probably leave his legs unprotected. Likewise, if the JKD practitioner wants to clinch, he can fake a low-line punch or takedown to encourage his opponent to expose his upper body.

- The key to being nontelegraphic lies in maintaining a poker face and a poker body. The JKD stylist does not reveal his intentions until he is ready to force his adversary to commit to a defense.

- When closing the gap for a clinch or takedown, the JKD practitioner pays attention to his opponent's perimeter. A boxer may allow him to get closer because he is used to fighting up close. A kicker may lash out from farther away because he is used to keeping distance between himself and his opponent. In either case, awareness is essential.

- To move into punching range without taking a boot to the belly, the JKD stylist is prepared to enter with a real or fake kick. Once in punching range, he may use a rapid combination to force his foe to cover up, thus opening a clear path to his legs.

- Another JKD ploy for closing the gap and getting into punching range involves trapping the opponent's lead arm before advancing.

- Against an aggressive opponent, the JKD fighter may prefer to use counterfighting. He will wait for his opponent to step forward with a jab or recover after a kick, then switch into slam-down mode.

- Once the JKD practitioner gets into tie-up range, he may not need to

Simple indirect attack: William Holland (left) squares off with an opponent (1). He executes a lead-hand eye jab to make the opponent shift his attention to his upper-body targets (2), then shoots in and seizes his leg (3). Holland immediately wraps his right leg around the other man's calf and pushes against his thigh (4) to force him to the ground (5). Once there, Holland can finish him with strikes or a lock.

go to the ground. His striking and infighting skills can enable him to use punches, elbow strikes, kicks, knee thrusts and head butts while minimizing the other man's ability to resist.

• The JKD fighter uses the concept of circumstantial spontaneity: Once he analyzes his opponent's physical ability, skill level and fighting style, he employs the way of attack that most efficiently overcomes the other man's defenses. Those ways of attack are outlined below.

Simple Direct Attack

• With respect to striking mode, Bruce Lee used to say, "When in doubt, hit." The same holds true for the type of close-range fighting that takes place in a clinch.

• If the JKD stylist has the advantage of size and power and is skilled at grappling, he may want to go directly for a takedown or submission hold. There will be little his opponent can do about it if he dives right in for a double-leg takedown and dumps his foe on his head, or if he climbs right into the mount and puts him out with an eye-popping stranglehold.

Simple Indirect Attack

• If the opponent is more skilled and less vulnerable, the JKD fighter will often progress to the indirect attack, which relies on feints for effectiveness.

• If he intends to shoot in with a single- or double-leg takedown, the JKD practitioner will set up his opponent as if he is planning to clinch or attack high. As soon as the opponent raises his guard, the JKD stylist will shoot for his legs.

• If the JKD stylist wants to clinch from the side, he will fake in the opposite direction. When the other man takes the bait and leans or moves in the desired direction, the JKD fighter will push him in the direction he just faked, then shoot in.

• On the ground, subtle movements and indications of movement can produce predictable reactions from an opponent who is susceptible to such tactics. The JKD stylist may aim a punch or palm strike at his face, and when the opponent reaches up to block or control the hand, the JKD stylist will seize the arm and lock it. If he wants to attack the neck, the martial artist will apply pressure to the eye socket or temple with his wrist bone or knuckle.

Attack by Combination

• The JKD practitioner who possesses good speed, power and endurance can use the principle of attack by combination as easily on the ground as he does on his feet.

• If the attacker tries to use a direct, penetrating move, the JKD student can counter it and, once the opportunity has passed, alter his orientation to strike a more accessible target. He executes a rapid succession of moves with speed, intensity and ferocity, overwhelming his opponent and forcing

Immobilization attack: Holland and his opponent face each other (1). Holland enters with a low-line jab, which the opponent blocks (2). The jeet kune do stylist follows up with a maiming technique aimed at the radial nerve on the forearm (3). While the opponent is still numb from the strike, Holland executes a left cross to the head (4) and a Thai kick to the leg (5). With his adversary stunned and off-balance, Holland takes his back and transitions to a choke (6).

111

Attack by drawing: The grappler prepares to attack Holland (1). Holland initiates a lead-hand jab to make the opponent think he has left his legs unprotected. The opponent ducks to avoid the punch, then shoots in for the expected takedown (2). The jeet kune do expert immediately raises his knee and smashes it into the other man's face (3). He then grabs his hair and issues a palm-heel strike to the nose (4).

him into defensive mode until he can gain an arm lock, choke, or as Lee used to say, anything that scores.

• While executing an attack sequence, the JKD stylist maintains his balance and readiness to negate a counter from his opponent.

Attack by Drawing

• During stand-up fighting, the JKD practitioner uses attack by drawing to lure his opponent in and counterattack or intercept him while he is launching his own assault. That works because most people tend to forget about their own defensive vulnerability when they smell blood.

• During a ground fight, the JKD practitioner can use attack by drawing just as productively. In a closely matched contest, he can gain the advantage by baiting his opponent into going for an arm or for position. When he does the expected, the JKD fighter exploits the opening that results when he inevitably extends himself or leaves a body part unprotected.

- When baiting his opponent, the JKD stylist needs a keen sense of timing, positioning and accuracy if he is to cut off the other man and sink in his own hook. Counterfighting is known as the art of masters and champions, and it is indeed a skill that takes much training and tactical knowledge. If it is used weakly or halfheartedly, it will leave the martial artist open to attack.

Immobilization Attack

- The JKD student knows that trapping or otherwise immobilizing his opponent's defensive tools can open an avenue to strike. He also knows that the immobilization attack is a highly developed skill that few people master.
- When the JKD fighter attempts to secure a position, lock or hold, his opponent will often defend himself by placing his hand or arm in the way. The action does not surprise the experienced practitioner.
- If the opponent uses his arm to obstruct the JKD stylist's movement,

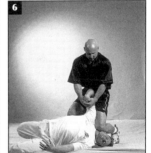

Not-so-simple direct attack: Holland assumes a fighting stance in front of a striker (1). Because Holland believes he has a grappling advantage, he launches a backhand strike (2) and a left cross (3), both of which the opponent nullifies. Holland then moves on to his true mission: to lock the opponent's lead arm (4) and force him to the ground (5). Once he falls, the jeet kune do practitioner ups the pressure he exerts on the trapped limb as he uses his knee to pin the other man's head to the floor (6).

the JKD stylist simply takes it out of play. He may use his body as a barrier to keep the hand from reaching its goal. If his body cannot be used, he may employ his arm to restrict the movement of his opponent's arm. That gives him a greater chance of securing a firm hold or strategic position, and it carries him one step closer to victory.

Make It Yours

It would be safe to say that most practitioners of *jeet kune do* and those martial artists who have delved into the wealth of insight provided by Bruce Lee's *Tao of Jeet Kune Do* have envisioned the ways of attack primarily from a striking perspective. I confess to having been guilty of the same offense.

For 24 years, the primary focus of my JKD training was on honing my punching and kicking skills. Although I had wrestled in high school and college, ground fighting stayed for the most part on the back burner in terms of time and effort invested.

Then along came Royce Gracie and the Ultimate Fighting Championship. Now I, like many martial artists around the world, can say I have spent the past several years mentally and physically dissecting the moves of Brazilian *jujutsu* and other ground-based systems to complement the strengths of Lee's progressive art. It has allowed me to develop "my own JKD," and it can do the same for you.

—W.H.

EXTREME SUBMISSION
4 Unconventional Grappling Techniques That Target the Upper Body

by Santos Flaniken and Robert W. Young • *Photos by Sara Fogan* • *June 2003*

Across the United States, Brazil, Japan and several other nations, amateur athletes are embracing an extreme sport known as mixed martial arts. They compete in hand-to-hand combat until a winner is determined by a knockout or a submission. They develop their skills by training at dedicated MMA camps and by studying boxing, wrestling, judo and *jujutsu*. They have watched their sport grow explosively over the past 10 years as more martial artists and members of the public catch on.

Virtually all MMA competitors now know by heart the techniques and strategies that would have guaranteed victory just a few short years ago. To prevail in the 21st century, a fighter must be prepared to take his opponent by surprise, and that is becoming more difficult every day. To help mixed martial artists stay on the cutting edge, this article will present four proven moves that anyone can use to target his opponent's upper body. The techniques are derived from various forms of jujutsu and the eclectic teachings of two master grapplers and members of the *Black Belt* Hall of Fame: Gene LeBell and Gokor Chivichyan.

Squeeze the neck: Santos Flaniken (top) assumes the scarf-hold position, trapping his opponent's head and right arm (1). As the opponent tries to escape by rolling to his left, Flaniken helps him with his left hand (2). He then places his left leg over the other man's head (3) and flexes it to put pressure on his neck (4).

115

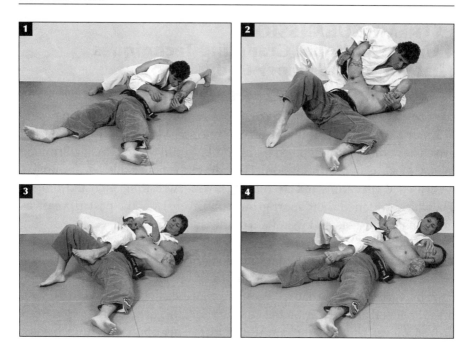

Wrench the arm: Flaniken pins his opponent's upper body to the mat (1). As soon as the opponent wraps his right arm around Flaniken's back, the grappling expert traps it under his arm and begins to shift his body (2). He places his leg on the opponent's thigh to keep him from escaping (3), then pushes the other man's face away while lifting with his hips to inflict pain on the shoulder and elbow (4).

Squeeze the Neck

Begin from judo's *kesa gatame* (scarf-hold position), which enables you to trap your opponent's head with your right arm and immobilize his right arm with your left hand. Your legs should be spread wide to maximize your base. Do not make the mistake of trying to submit him at this point. The position is intended to control him while he struggles and eventually runs out of gas.

Before he becomes too exhausted to continue, however, he will probably try to escape by rolling to his left. Let him do so. In fact, assist him by using your left hand to push his right arm away from you. Once he is on his side, throw your left leg over his head and trap it. Allow your body weight to pin him to the mat. Flex your left leg to apply pressure on his neck. Use your left hand to push downward on his right arm, which contributes an opposing force and augments the power of your leg. If you are large enough in relation to him, key-lock your left foot behind your right knee for a quicker submission.

Wrench the Arm

Start in a position that is similar to what judo practitioners refer to as the *kuzure kami shiho gatame* (broken upper-locking-of-four-quarters position). Wait until your opponent extends his right arm up and around your back. Trap that limb under your right arm and, if necessary, grasp his triceps with your hand. Then swing your outside (left) leg under your inside leg until you are lying on your back parallel to him. Drape your left leg across his right leg to keep him from rolling and escaping. To attack his trapped arm, simply lift with your hips. The pain can be amplified by using your free hand to shove his face away from the source of the action.

The key to successfully executing this move lies in the delicate manner in which you hold his trapped elbow. Because your power comes from your hips, there is no need to clutch it like a football. If you do everything correctly, your hip lift will dislocate his shoulder and elbow, but he will probably tap long before then.

Lock the Arms

Begin in the scarf-hold position with your right arm around your opponent's neck and your left hand controlling his right elbow to prevent him from punching you. If you need an extra hand hold, grab your pant leg with your right hand or curl your fingers around your thigh. Next, use your

Lock the arms: From the scarf-hold position (1), Flaniken maneuvers his opponent's arm downward and traps it under his right leg (2). He then locks his right foot behind his left knee for added security (3). To apply pressure, he lifts with his hips, but if that is not enough to submit the opponent, he can lock his left arm, as well (4).

Scissor the head: Flaniken mounts his opponent and prepares for an armbar (1). He then swings his body to the side and takes the trapped arm with him, but the opponent manages to get his head out from under Flaniken's left leg (2). The grappler immediately repositions his right foot against the opponent's neck, slides his right arm under the other man's right leg and re-establishes his hold on the trapped arm (3). Next, Flaniken places his left leg on the opponent's neck to complete the scissor choke while he hyperextends the trapped arm (4).

left arm to angle his right arm downward until you can swing your right leg over it. Bend it to secure your hold on his limb and key-lock your foot behind your left knee. Lift with your hips to put pressure on his trapped arm. In all likelihood, he will tap immediately.

If the opponent is really flexible, he may be able to endure the odd angle at which you have torqued his arm. You should then snake your right arm under his left shoulder and grab his wrist. A bit of outward pressure is all it takes to induce pain in that arm, as well. If it still is not enough, use your left hand to pull his head toward his chest.

Scissor the Head

Begin from the mount position. Use your left hand to pin your opponent's right arm against your chest and your right palm to push his face to his left. Rotate your hips around his shoulder and lean backward to execute a traditional cross-body armbar. If he manages to get his head out from under your left leg, immediately reposition your right leg so the arch of your foot is pressed against the back of his neck. Simultaneously slide your right arm under his right leg and bend it until you can grasp his trapped arm. Then place your left leg across the top of his neck to perform a scissor choke. Maintain the armbar and the hold on his right leg so he is attacked from a variety of angles. If necessary, you can release your grip on his arm and lock his right foot.

Trickling Down

It has been said that the martial arts have evolved more in the past decade than they have in the past millennium. In large part that is because of the discoveries the top MMA athletes are making in the gym and the ring. The best part is that the unprecedented access all martial artists have to their findings means that every new technique and strategy the pros use eventually trickles down to amateur competitors and self-defense enthusiasts. All that is required to assimilate their methods is an open mind.

When the Going Gets Tough ...

In combat—whether in a tournament or on the street—executing a single technique on your opponent can be difficult. If that opponent possesses fighting skills that are equal to yours, the challenge can be even greater. In such a situation, your chances of victory can be increased through the use of "baiting."

Baiting techniques come in two varieties: The first makes your opponent think a certain, obvious move is coming, then when he blocks it, you finish him with something completely unexpected. The second offers him a disguised chance to attack you, and when he takes it, you submit him with a finishing hold. Either way it's entrapment, pure and simple.

True baiting is often ignored during the heat of battle. For one reason or another, combatants usually fail to think about using their body to trap their opponent. Consequently, they tend to plunge ahead using unnecessary brute strength to accomplish their objective. But experienced martial artists know it's wiser to use less force and conserve their energy for when they really need it. Likewise, they know it's better to remain loose and pliable while they are trying to determine their opponent's weaknesses. But once they find it, they pounce.

—S.F.

GROUND FIGHTER'S GUIDE
How to Turn Sport Grappling Into Street Grappling

by Jeff Clancy and Jim Wagner • August 2003

The ground is the last place you want to be during a real fight. If you end up down there, it usually indicates that your stand-up battle plan failed catastrophically. Once you're flat on terra firma, you'll be forced to give up several key tactical advantages that you would normally have on your feet: mobility, varied avenues of escape, long-range striking capabilities and frequently the element of offense.

With so many limiting factors associated with ground fighting, why is everyone making such a fuss about it? Is it worth devoting your time, money and energy to learn this skill? In a word, yes.

History of Grappling

Ground fighting is nothing new. Egyptian and Chinese stone reliefs from around 3,000 B.C. depict combatants on the ground vying for positional dominance or a submission. A popular Greek theme found on pottery and bronze statues dating from 300 B.C. shows intertwined wrestlers. Four hundred years later, the Romans perfected the ground techniques that Westerners now learn in high school: Greco-Roman wrestling.

Half a world away, a Japanese professor named Jigoro Kano founded the art of judo in 1880. Not long afterward, it was adopted by the Japanese

Littering your training area with "clean" debris can mimic the conditions under which you might have to grapple on the street.

army and taught in schools throughout Japan. After World War II, judo migrated to the United States, where it became popular in the late 1940s and '50s.

Ground fighting has withstood the test of time, and many modern martial arts include some form of grappling. Today's students are not only discovering ground fighting but also are witnessing its renaissance. This rebirth started in 1993 when Royce Gracie, a *jujutsu* practitioner from Brazil, snatched the world's attention by winning the first Ultimate Fighting Championship. He went on to win the UFC 2, once again proving that a smaller, weaker person could beat a larger, stronger opponent on the ground. As a result of his victories, grappling schools sprang up around the world.

Most Fights Go Down

This renewed focus on ground tactics has had a positive impact on the martial arts. It has forced instructors and practitioners alike to rethink the reality of combat, which had been largely glossed over during the past two decades. The reality is that 75 percent of all civilian street fights end up on the ground, and almost 95 percent of all law-enforcement and institutional fights (jails, prisons, booking facilities) end up going down. Officials deliberately take the fight to the ground to control and arrest resisting subjects.

Although more people are aware of these facts, surprisingly few reality-based ground-fighting programs exist. Much of what is being taught is

When police officers learn how to fight on the ground, they must pay attention to weapons retention as well as to methods for defending against empty-hand attacks.

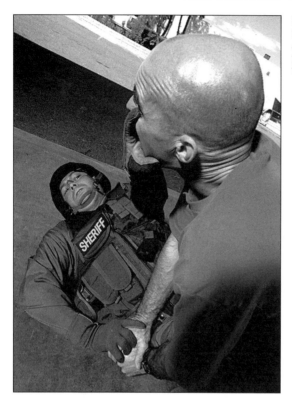

Most grappling training is unrealistic because it does not include defense against eye gouges, the authors say, yet such techniques are quite likely to be used on the street.

sport-oriented. Most systems have evolved into a sport or follow sportlike rules. A case in point is Brazilian jujutsu. According to 62-year-old instructor Ricardo Murgel of the Brazilian Jiu-Jitsu Federation, the majority of what is taught today is sport jujutsu. Consequently, it has little relevance to actual self-defense.

"A lot of people think that Brazilian jujutsu is combat, but what is being taught today is not what Carlos and Helio Gracie originally designed," Murgel said. "In the early days they taught strikes, chokes and down-and-dirty ground fighting—things that would not be allowed today in the sport. What is being marketed today is what we call 'submission fighting.' It's a sport. There are rules. Many schools claim to be realistic, but if you take a careful look, they're not for the street."

Although there are many similarities between the sporting arts and real combat, the sporting arts lack the additional tactics that make them effective in survival situations. It is similar to the differences that exist between a competition shooter and a combat soldier. Both practice on the range, regularly hitting targets. But who is more mentally prepared for targets that shoot back? Indeed, the competition shooter may be an expert marksman, plinking away at stationary targets or clay pigeons, but what happens when he has to push through an obstacle course with a full combat load, use cover and concealment, and fire from a less-than-ideal shooting position?

If there are very few reality-based programs out there, that must mean that most practitioners are learning ground tactics from sport-oriented systems. That is not to say that anything coming out of those schools won't help you in a real fight. On the contrary, sport-oriented arts lay a solid foundation for realistic ground fighting. If your current system already includes good basics, moving ahead to the next step of reality-based ground fighting will not be much of a leap for you.

Fantasy or Reality

To determine whether your system is really street-oriented, here are common characteristics of sport grappling:

- You are in an environment that is comfortable and predictable.
- You choose the time of day you train.
- You chose to go to the ground.
- You usually know who your partner is.
- You know how long you will grapple.
- You grapple on mats.
- You wear light protective gear.
- You do not strike, bite or eye-gouge.
- You do not risk serious injury by your partner.
- You are not injured.
- You do not have to defend against a weapon.
- You do not face multiple attackers.
- You do not roll with a drug user.
- You do not wear clothing that hinders your movements.
- You rest and drink water between rounds.
- You control your emotions because it's only training.
- You do not have to protect friends or loved ones.
- You can tap out whenever you want.

This list is by no means comprehensive, but it provides a basis for analysis, introspection and debate.

The next list, modified from the one listed above, will convey the reality of grappling on the street:

- You are in an environment that is unknown, unpredictable and possibly uncomfortable.
- You have no choice as to the time of day the fight occurs.
- You did not choose to go to the ground.
- You have no idea who your attacker is in most cases, and you are unaware of his strengths and weaknesses.
- You don't know how long the fight will last.
- You're grappling on a hard, "contaminated" surface such as asphalt, concrete, dirt or sand—and it may not be level.
- You have no protective gear.
- Your attacker can strike, bite and eye-gouge.
- You're attacker is attempting to injure or kill you.
- You may have sustained a serious injury.
- You may face a weapon.
- You may face multiple attackers.
- You may face an attacker who is under the influence of a mind-altering substance such as alcohol or drugs.
- You are wearing clothing that inhibits your movements (jacket, torn shirt, ballistic vest, wet clothes, etc.).
- You have little or no opportunity to rest, and you are losing fluids fast.
- You are starting to lose emotional control as panic and pain set in.
- You have friends or loved ones whom you must protect.
- You absolutely cannot tap out.

Making the Transition

Possessing the most effective ground-fighting tactics is not just a matter of taking your current program and going harder or adding a few punches and kicks to your existing skills. Rather, it involves restructuring all aspects of your training to make it better resemble the second list. Because that's easier said than done, you will need to make a third list that will give you tangible building blocks to construct a new program you can implement at your current training site.

Although in a real conflict you will probably fight on a hard surface, you still need to train on mats or other soft surfaces for safety. However, instead of always laying the mats out flat, put them on a plywood slope or place items such as kicking shields and boxing gloves under them to make a bumpy, uneven surface. Another option is to cover your mats with sandbox sand, party ice or other sterile debris (empty plastic bottles, newspapers, used clothes, etc.). By adding "garnish" to your mats, you provide a greater degree of realism and learn how to fight on contaminated surfaces.

Military operators and cops frequently train in low-light scenarios, and you should do the same because most violent crimes occur at night. When practicing your grappling techniques, try turning the lights out or at least dimming them to simulate a dark alley, nightclub or your home in the middle of the night.

Wear what you'll fight in. If you're a cop, security guard, soldier, ambulance driver or other professional who is subject to altercations, practice ground fighting in full gear: ballistic vest, gun belt, boots, etc. If you're a civilian who lives in a cold climate, try your techniques while wearing a winter coat, gloves and a hat. If you train only in comfortable workout clothes, you might be handicapped when a real situation arises. By wearing the clothing you will most likely fight in, you will quickly discover which parts of your gear get caught and which restrict your movement.

Practicing strikes from the ground is just as important as learning

Wearing a boxing glove and holding a rubber knife, Jim Wagner (right) prepares to attack Jeff Clancy (1). As Wagner slashes with the knife (2), Clancy intercepts the blow by kicking away the attacker's hand (3).

them from a standing position. Most good rape-prevention courses start by teaching students how to fight from the ground up. Why? Because the ground—a bed, car seat, floor, etc.—is where the victim will quickly find herself in a real sexual assault. So why not start from the place where most of the fighting is done? The same holds true in ground-fighting courses. Learn to strike from your back and both sides. Use focus gloves, kicking shields and other striking devices.

Incorporate strikes into freestyle matches. Whenever you train on the ground, do not limit your striking techniques. Obviously, contact should be light or simulated, but it must be done to promote muscle memory. Protective gear can also be worn to protect the attacker whenever you practice eye gouges, throat grabs and groin squeezes.

Use training weapons made of rubber, plastic or foam. Start on the ground, with you and your partner placing your hands on the same rubber gun or rubber knife. A third person calls, "Go!" and the two of you struggle for the weapon. Or you can engage in a grappling match until your partner pulls out a concealed training knife. Then you must defend against his attacks. Such realistic training scenarios teach you to keep your eyes open at all times and make you deal immediately with the realities that

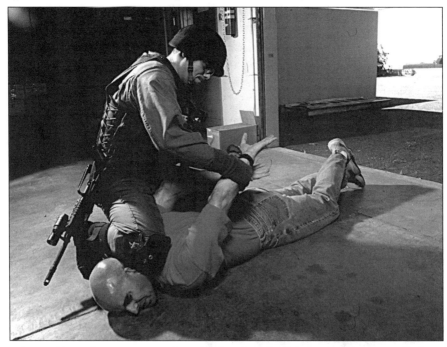

Military and law-enforcement personnel are often forced to fight while wearing up to 20 pounds of gear, the authors say. Consequently, their training should be done while wearing the same equipment.

THE ULTIMATE GUIDE TO GRAPPLING

can occur on the ground.

How do you simulate grappling with a person who is high on drugs? You make sure that your attacker is fresh and rested before a match, while you do calisthenics or run until you're exhausted. Then you return to the mat to grapple with your energized opponent. This simulates the edge that a person will have when he is under the influence.

Try taking on multiple attackers while you're on the ground. The thought is scary, but you have to train for it. If you want to see whether your current ground tactics can get you out of a bad situation, go against two opponents. Put on a helmet and give your attackers the option of kicking you in the head—using light contact only. You may find that one attacker will hold you while the other kicks you in the head or punches you. It is a situation you may end up in if gang members ever jump you. You will learn that the key to survival lies in using fast and effective techniques to get to your feet as soon as possible. In a real fight, you cannot afford to roll around on the ground.

How do you simulate injuries and learn how to keep pressing on in spite of them? There is a crude but effective method: As you and your opponent grapple, a third person pours ice water over both of you when you least expect it. The sudden shock of the extreme cold simulates the instantaneous shock you would experience if you were wounded. Your breathing becomes rapid and shallow, your clothes get wet (as they would from blood and sweat) and your muscles tense. To prevail, you will need to develop the will to survive.

Final Advice

We have supplied you with the blueprint for turning your sport-grappling workouts into an effective combat course. To summarize, remember the words of Ricardo Murgel: "The only way you're going to change your sport grappling into combat grappling is to know what the criminals are learning. You have to train realistically with rubber guns and knives in plain clothes, and learn to use the environment to your advantage. The American writer John Steinbeck once said, 'The final weapon is the brain.' You need a combat mind-set, or else all your techniques will fail."

FIGHTING FROM THE BOTTOM
5 Techniques for Submitting an Opponent Held in Your Guard

by S.D. Seong • September 2003

Grapplers call it the "guard." It occurs whenever one person lies on his back and gains control over his opponent by putting him between his legs. The bottom person's legs may or may not be locked together at the ankles.

You have probably seen fighters use the guard in the Ultimate Fighting Championship and Japan's PRIDE and Pancrase extravaganzas, as well as here in the pages of *Black Belt*. But if you have not trained extensively in grappling, you may have been left wondering how two participants can go about attacking and defending from this strange position in which most hand and foot strikes fail to function.

Defending Yourself

As a grappler, you probably shouldn't plan on maneuvering into the guard to attack your foe. But if a quick opponent manages to shoot in and take you down, you should not mind being on bottom temporarily. For this reason, the guard is often classified as a defensive posture.

That does not mean your opponent cannot attempt to attack while you hold him between your legs, however. In fact, he may try any number of techniques, and some of them may succeed if you are not prepared.

Perhaps the first thought of an opponent caught in your guard involves grabbing your groin. After all, everything is right there, a mere couple of inches from his itchy fingers. A bit *too* inviting, perhaps? You bet, because once your opponent diverts his attention from his defense to your groin, you can easily trap an arm for an armbar or other finishing technique.

The next most common attack is probably the downward punch to the face. You should prepare yourself for this possibility by keeping your head off the ground. That increases mobility and, if you do get punched, results in an impact with considerably less force than if you had kept your head against the ground. But as soon as the attacker commits himself to a punch, he once again exposes his arm, which can easily end up getting broken or wrenched out of its socket.

While held close to your chest, your opponent may try to throw a series of short hook punches to the side of your head. Because the power of his hips and shoulders cannot be used to amplify the power of his striking arm, these hits will serve mostly to distract you. Nevertheless, they can inflict some damage—just look at Royce Gracie's head after the UFC 5.

Another attack consists of your closely held opponent sliding forward along your body to deliver a head butt to the bottom of your chin. You may have seen Ken Shamrock use this technique against Gracie in their superfight at the UFC 5. The head butt can definitely take its toll on your jaw, but you can easily block it with your hand or avoid it by turning your head to either side.

Clear for Attack

Fighting offensively with your opponent in your guard works well because you have four weapons—two arms and two legs—while he has only two. And you can play a waiting game until he tires out and becomes vulnerable, or until he tries something and gives you an opening for a finishing technique.

Two attacks are common: If he allows you to trap one of his arms, you may be able to catch him in a triangle choke. If he places one arm on the ground near your torso, you can grasp it at the wrist, twist your body and encircle his upper arm with your other arm, which results in what Brazilian-*jujutsu* practitioners call a *kimura*.

The additional offensive techniques discussed below come from the

As Gokor Chivichyan (left) holds Karo Parisyan in his open guard (1), the opponent tries to stand (2). Chivichyan hooks the opponent's left ankle with his right hand, pushes him backward with his left leg (3) and sits up to secure his hold on the leg (4). Chivichyan then wraps his right arm around the ankle and leans backward to twist the foot to the outside (5).

Chivichyan holds Sarkis Chivitchian in his open guard (1). The opponent moves his right leg in preparation to escape, and Chivichyan inserts his left leg between his legs (2). He then pushes the opponent to the side as he places his left calf in the crook of his left knee (3). Next, Chivichyan sits up and forces the other man down (4). He hooks his left foot behind his own right knee and pulls the opponent's lower leg to apply the lock (5).

arsenal of Gokor Chivichyan, a 39-year-old grappling expert originally from Armenia. Chivichyan started training in combat *sambo* at age 5 and later took up judo, Western boxing and *shotokan* karate. He became the bare-knuckle combat-sambo champion of the Soviet Union five times, judo champion of Europe two times and sport-sambo champion of the world two times.

Chivichyan now operates the Hayastan Dojo in Hollywood, California, and has trained one of the most successful judo teams in the United States. Not content merely to coach martial artists, the *Black Belt* Hall of Fame member recently brought home two gold medals in judo from the Pacific Northwest World Festival. He offers the following proven techniques as a complement to your basic grappling skills.

As Rufi Keshishyan (right) tries to pass Chivichyan's guard, Chivichyan grabs his left collar with his left hand (1). He then reaches for the other side of the collar to complete the cross-lapel choke (2). However, the opponent keeps it out of reach. Chivichyan immediately shifts his body and pulls the other man's right arm to the side (3). He places his right leg over the opponent's head and shoulder (4) and pulls the collar as he pushes with his legs (5).

Ankle Twist

As you keep your opponent in your guard, he may try to escape by standing up. Whether he manages to plant two feet or only one, a basic ankle twist can quickly bring him back down to the mat and elicit a break or submission.

"Most people will stand up and push down with their elbows to try to pass the guard," Chivichyan says. As your opponent pushes against your stomach to raise himself, trap his hands or elbows.

"Then circle your right arm around his left heel and pull it toward your armpit," Chivichyan says. At the same time, move your left leg onto his torso and use it to push him backward and down.

"Make sure his heel is [against] your rib cage," Chivichyan continues. The intense pressure of the lock comes from twisting the trapped foot with your right forearm. Once he is on his back, hit him with a heel kick to the

While held in the open guard, Arthur Chivichyan prepares to punch Gokor (1). The sambo instructor places his right knee across the boy's chest to create space (2), then uses his left hand to trap the boy's right wrist and places his right forearm against the right side of his neck (3). Next, he shifts the opponent's right arm across his body and pins him close (4). The senior Chivichyan circles his left arm behind the opponent's head and grasps his right wrist to complete the choke (5).

chest or face, but the pressure from twisting his foot should prove more than enough to stop him.

Leg Lock

A simple leg lock can come into play when your opponent is in your guard and tries to push one of your legs down so he can pass over it and mount you. Grab his uniform so you can control his body, then slip your left leg past his right knee and lock it around his left knee. At the same time, hold his right arm at the biceps so he cannot punch you.

"Use your right knee to push his left arm away from its position on your thigh," Chivichyan says. "Then push his left arm across [your body] and to the floor. Use your left arm to go over his back, lock your left foot behind your right knee and pull on his left foot." This applies severe pressure to his knee using a figure-4 leg position.

Lapel Choke

If your opponent happens to be wearing a sturdy article of clothing—such as a uniform or jacket—two simple chokes may work against him. First is the basic cross-lapel choke: Put one hand across his neck, then slide it in deep and grab the collar—the farther back, the better. Your other hand reaches toward the opposite side of his neck, passing over the arm of your planted hand, and grasps the collar on the opposite side. Apply pressure on the arteries in his neck by keeping your wrists straight and moving your elbows away from each other.

Yet a skilled opponent can easily prevent you from reaching the second collar, Chivichyan says. "In that case, do the technique holding onto his arm, and he won't know what you are doing." After trapping his right wrist, shift the arm across his neck. You now have choking surfaces on both sides of his neck: your forearm on the left side and his own right arm on the right.

Next, place your right leg over his head and push. Pull on his trapped right arm for added effect.

Carotid Attack

The next technique closes off the carotid arteries on the sides of your opponent's neck. Start by putting your knee on his chest, then extend your right hand across his body and grasp his right shoulder. "At the same time, your left hand holds his right wrist," Chivichyan says. "Then move your knee away from his chest—you don't need it there because you're no longer concerned about getting punched." This action will allow his body to lie directly on top of yours.

You now have him locked close so he cannot move. Use your left hand to circle his neck and grab his right wrist. Then lock your right hand over your left forearm or on his shoulder. That action constricts the arteries on both sides of his neck.

Precise placement of your arms is not as critical as in some other techniques. "There's no need to worry if his chin is down because you don't choke him there," Chivichyan says. "You are cutting off the blood going through the carotid arteries on the side.

"Even if you don't have a uniform on, it works 100 percent. Without a uniform, you can grab his neck and hold your own arm."

Arm Lock

If your opponent tries to strike you while in your guard, you can easily take advantage of the extended limb. "When a punch comes in, block it and trap his elbow," Chivichyan says. Once restrained, that elbow lends itself to several types of locks, one of which—the rolling-elbow lock—is described below.

Not surprisingly, the key lies in "rolling" your opponent's elbow. As you extend your arm past the elbow of his trapped arm, you must "scrape" it along the joint to rotate it until the crook faces the direction in which you want to apply pressure—and keep it there. Otherwise, you will not be able to prevent him from bending his arm and escaping.

Once his elbow is rolled and locked, lock your left hand on your right forearm or right thigh to increase the pressure. "You don't have to grab anything," Chivichyan says. "You just push his chin away and squeeze his body between your knees." His arm is trapped and locked, and his body is prevented from twisting and escaping.

Softening Him Up

If your opponent seems to have too much balance and defensive composure for your chokes and locks to succeed from your bottom position, you can always try one of the four distraction tactics frequently seen in the UFC: short chopping heel strikes to the kidney areas, repeated punches to the floating ribs, palm strikes to the side of the head or ears, or elbow smashes to the collarbone. These may encourage your opponent to direct some of his attention to protecting those irritated parts of his body—perhaps just long enough for you to complete a finishing technique.

As Parisyan punches, Chivichyan places his right knee on his chest to keep him away (1-2). He then blocks the strike with his left arm (3) and uses that arm to "roll" the opponent's elbow counterclockwise and trap it (4). Next, Chivichyan locks his left hand on his right thigh and uses his right hand to push the opponent's head away, thus increasing the pressure on the elbow (5).

Of course, he can always treat you to some of the same medicine—or to some of that described at the beginning of this article. But if you have conditioned your body well enough and have learned how to take a hit, you should be able to weather this relatively minor storm. And if you have practiced your grappling techniques for fighting on your back, you will be able to wait for the right moment and slap on just the right choke, leg lock or arm lock to win the confrontation.

TWISTED TECHNIQUES
Catch-as-Catch-Can Wrestling Descended From the Original No-Holds-Barred Fighting Art

by Chuck Hustmyre • Photos courtesy of Tony Cecchin • December 2003

"A hundred years ago, every wrestler in the country knew submission holds," says Tony Cecchine, the world's leading exponent of catch-as-catch-can wrestling. Today, however, safety concerns have resulted in dangerous techniques such as joint locks, strikes and chokes having been removed from the sport.

Catch-as-catch-can wrestling has not only retained those techniques but also has honed them into effective weapons. "What we do is the antithesis of sport," Cecchine says. "We teach people to be as brutal as possible. We don't teach them how to score points. We teach them self-defense."

Ancient Ways

Catch wrestling's roots are as old as unarmed combat itself. The 4,000-year-old sculptures in the Egyptian tomb at Beni Hassan show wrestlers performing holds and takedowns, including a throw in which one fighter drops to his back, plants his foot in his opponent's stomach and hurls him over his head. Thousands of years later, that technique became judo's *tomoenage*, or stomach throw.

In 648 B.C., the Greeks introduced into the Olympic Games a violent form of wrestling called *pankration*. It soon became the most popular Olympic competition. The combatants began on their feet—much like modern wrestlers—and their goal was to force their opponent to submit. Striking, kicking, sweeping, choking and joint-locking were all acceptable. Even vicious foot and leg holds, considered too risky for regular Greek wrestling, were permitted.

Fast-forward a couple thousand years. In the late 1800s and early 1900s, long before the theatrics that now pass as pro wrestling, carnivals traveled the United States, carrying with them wrestlers who would take on all comers. The greats—men like Frank Gotch, George Tragos and Lou Thesz—were known as "hookers."

"A hook is a crippling submission hold designed to maim or break something on an opponent," Cecchine explains. Today, few have the stomach for such brutal fighting techniques and the training needed to perfect them.

A good percentage of those few purists who *do* have the stomach for it have sought out Cecchine and catch wrestling. The grappler doesn't kid

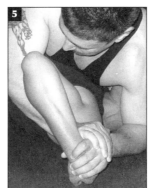

Top wrist lock: The technique begins with the opponent on his back and the catch wrestler on top in the cross-chest position (1). The wrestler uses his right arm to "monitor" his adversary's left elbow as he controls the limb (2). He then uses his left hand to twist the other man's trapped wrist as he angles it toward the mat and rakes his right elbow across his face (3). After inserting his right arm under the opponent's arm and locking his fingers onto his left wrist, the wrestler lifts as he moves his right elbow toward the center of the opponent's body (4-5).

them: Learning how to fight is hard work, and it takes years to get good at it. It comes down to personal commitment, he insists. "Do you want to be very tough, or do you just want something to do two nights a week?"

Hundreds of techniques make up the catch-wrestling arsenal: hand strikes, kicks, takedowns, sweeps, gouges, arm locks, leg locks, torso cranks, neck cranks, chokes, rips and so on. Most of them can be executed while either standing or on the ground. But fighting is not about the number of techniques you know, Cecchine says. Boxers may know only a few moves, but they have mastered them. Catch wrestlers pick the techniques they like best, then become experts at them. "To master the bare essence of wrestling, that's probably 10 to 12 techniques," he says.

The following are some prime examples of what separates catch wrestling from other grappling arts. Although the concepts may seem familiar, that's where the similarities end. As you study the techniques, Cecchine advises you to develop your awareness of the art's "unnatural position" theory, in which you employ a twisting technique to force your opponent's body into an unnatural—and incredibly painful—orientation.

Top Wrist Lock

Catch wrestling's top wrist lock simultaneously assaults the opponent's wrist, elbow and shoulder. "A street fight is fast and furious," Cecchine says. "If you find yourself on the ground, you're going to want to end it quickly, and one way to do that is to snap your opponent's wrist, dislocate his elbow or tear apart his shoulder."

There are dozens of variations of the technique, but Cecchine says it's more important to understand the basic method. Start with your opponent on his back and assume the cross-chest position with your head toward his left side. Have him raise his left arm in a defensive position.

As soon as his arm is up, use your right arm to "monitor" his elbow by keeping it under the joint. With your left hand, grab his left wrist and twist as you swing it over his shoulder. Don't use a thumbless grip. Notice that his pinkie is facing him and his palm is facing the ground. Later, when you bring his hand to the mat, his wrist will still be in that position.

"The twist is vital," Cecchine says. "It places him in an unnatural and very painful position." The tendons and muscles in his forearm will be misaligned, and his strength will be almost entirely taken away.

From there, use your hips and body for power as you drive his hand to the floor and his elbow next to his side. Don't fight his strength. To make sure you're using proper technique and leverage, keep your elbows close to your body at all times. Press down on him to keep him from rolling out.

To finish him, move your right elbow directly up, along his ribs and toward the center of his body. Try not to move it in the direction of his hips. Crank it inch by inch so he can submit before his wrist, shoulder and elbow are torn apart.

Front Face Lock

Going to the ground is not always the best option. Sometimes the ground itself is dangerous because of gravel, rough asphalt or broken bottles. Sometimes you're facing more than one opponent. Fortunately, catch wrestling is not a one-dimensional art. It includes methods for choking a man and cranking his neck whether he's on his knees or on his feet. The front face lock is one of them.

Start in a referee's position, with your right hand on the outside of your opponent's right arm and his left hand cupped around his neck. Immediately pop your head straight up. At the same time, clear his left arm from the side of his neck and start sliding your left arm across the left side of his face.

Two important things need to happen now: First, you must get his head twisted. As noted above, a nice grind or strike across the face will help get the job done. The farther his head twists, the more pressure there is on his neck. Second, you need to place the back of your right wrist on his trapezius muscle or deltoid and lock your fingers together. Keep your elbows in

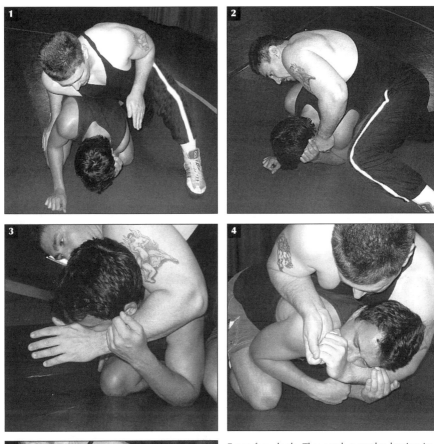

Front face lock: The catch wrestler begins in a referee's position on top of his opponent (1). After lifting his head, the wrestler wedges his left arm between the adversary's left hand and head (2). His left arm then grinds across the face of the opponent as he starts twisting his head (3). Once he has positioned the back of his right wrist on the other man's shoulder, the wrestler locks his fingers, trapping the head between his arm and chest (4). By increasing the torsional pressure and shifting his legs, the wrestler can effect a submission in the ring or an incapacitation on the street (5).

tight as you crank, and make sure the pressure is sufficient to cause some serious pain. In practice, he will tap out with the slightest force, but in a street fight, you can break his neck with minimal force. Use caution.

Rips

"Ripping is savage and brutal," Cecchine says. In catch-wrestling terms, it's about striking, gouging and attacking pressure points. In a fight, there are good and bad times to attempt a rip. Your likelihood of succeeding depends in part on the level of resistance you're encountering.

"If the guy's a fish, and he lets you get him in a top wrist lock, the fight's over," Cecchine explains. "You don't need to rip him. But if he wants to be a tough guy, then you've got to rip him."

Almost all fights end in a clinch, he says, and most of them wind up on the ground. In such situations, you won't have room to throw ordinary punches and kicks. If you're not prepared, you'll be hanging on for dear

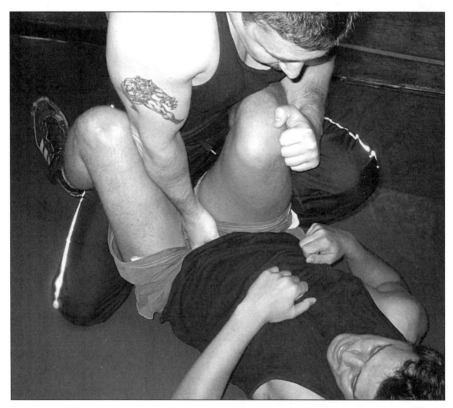

In catch wrestling, ripping is the term used to describe striking, gouging and other unconventional techniques that facilitate grappling maneuvers. Here, a groin shot helps a wrestler set up a leg lock.

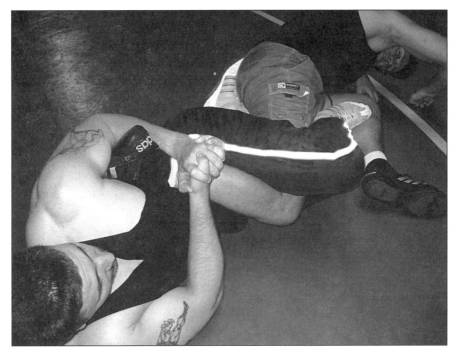

Twisting a body part into an unnatural position plays a central role in many of catch wrestling's techniques, including the heel hook.

life. Obviously, you need to have a plan, and even more important, you need to have practiced your plan.

That's where ripping comes in. It's vicious, but it'll end a fight in a heartbeat.

Rips to the Head
• **The mouth:** Secure your opponent's head with one arm, then shove your finger or thumb into his mouth and hook his cheek. Make sure you get your digit between his cheek and teeth, not between his upper and lower teeth. As soon as you start pulling, he'll either give up or feel his flesh tear.

• **The nose:** Use your palm to push the pliable tip to one side, then drive the stiff cartilage upward.

• **The ear:** Plunge a finger as deep as you can get it into the ear canal. It not only will cause excruciating pain but also will act as a handle for twisting his head.

- **The eye:** Attack from the outside corner, not the tear duct. Always use caution in training, and employ the real technique only in extreme circumstances.

Rips to the Body
- **The liver:** Located to the right of the opponent's navel, it's big and painful when attacked. Remember the adage: Throw a left for the liver. Hit the organ with a left uppercut. In a clinch, dig your elbow into it. On the ground, work it with your knee.
- **The ribs:** Grind them with your elbows and knees.
- **The armpits:** Drive your fingers into them until he quits.
- **The collarbone:** Pretend it's a handle and grab it. Dig your fingers or thumb into it, or strike it and try to break it.
- **The upper arm:** There's a spot on the inside of your opponent's arm, between the biceps and triceps, that you can bore into and actually hit bone. It's not a fight-stopper, but it'll help you move his limb.

Pressure Points
- **Under the nose:** Drive the edge of your hand under his nose. Push up and back, toward the top of his head.
- **Below the ear:** Jab the tip of your thumb or finger into the notch between his jaw and neck. Push like you're trying to make it come out through his nostril.
- **Under the jaw:** Hook your thumb into the soft spot halfway between the tip of his chin and his throat, then claw the lower part of his face with your fingers.

No Mercy
If those techniques sound harsh, it's because they are. Catch wrestling isn't a sport. It is combat, up close and personal. If you're willing to work hard and your ego and body can take the punishment, it's likely to be the best form of unarmed combat that will ever stand between you and a severe beating or even death.

CERTAIN VICTORY
4 Tried-and-True Submissions Techniques From Master Grappler Gokor Chivichyan

by Robert W. Young and Ed Pollard • Photos by Rick Hustead • April 2004

In the sports world, there are two types of experts: those who win and those who teach them how to win.

Those who win always seem to get the lion's share of publicity, but when a coach leads athlete after athlete to victory, doesn't he also deserve some accolades? We think so. That's why *Black Belt* and *FightSport* are bringing you this article showcasing the awesome grappling talents of Gokor Chivichyan, a man who continues to lead the best of the best to the most prestigious winner's circles in the martial arts world.

It all began when the top competitors in the Ultimate Fighting Championship and PRIDE started hearing rumors of a grappling legend from Armenia. Skilled in judo and *sambo* and tutored by the legendary Gene LeBell, he quickly gained a reputation for knowing thousands of ground-fighting techniques and for being able to deftly teach any one of them—along with numerous counters to it—to anybody. "More and more people started coming here to train with me," Chivichyan says. "Because most of them were strikers, they wanted to learn how to grapple. I taught them how to enter, how to catch their opponent and how to take him down."

Since those early days, scores of bigwigs have signed up for private lessons at Chivichyan's Hayastan Dojo in Hollywood, California. "I don't want to mention their names because I don't know if they would feel comfortable with it," he says. "I'll just say, it's most of the champions. They come from all over the United States and Europe. And I'm happy because it looks like we're doing something right."

Just what does Chivichyan give those elite athletes to keep them salivating for more? "I use my experience to teach them what I know," says the 40-year-old martial artist. "It starts with judo, sambo and wrestling, and moves on to what I'm doing now, which is way beyond that technically."

The following four sequences, which take you step by step from the entry to the takedown to the submission, are among Chivichyan's favorites for technically dispensing with the toughest opponents.

Rear Lapel Choke

As a grappler in the 21st century, you need to know more than just finishing holds, Chivichyan says. That's why he emphasizes learning the

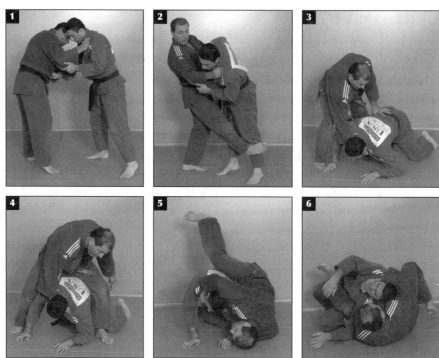

Rear lapel choke: Gokor Chivichyan (left) grabs his opponent's lapel and sleeve (1), then pulls him off-balance as he sweeps his left shin (2). When the man falls, Chivichyan places his hand on his back while keeping his grip on the lapel (3). Next, he puts his leg across the opponent's back and grabs his pants (4). Chivichyan then dives over his back (5), taking the man with him (6). When they stop rolling, he executes the lapel choke (7).

setup to a technique as much as the technique itself. Before you can use a proven fight-stopper such as the rear lapel choke, you must close the gap and go to the ground, he says.

Begin by using your right hand to grasp your opponent's left lapel and your left hand to hold his right sleeve. Immediately pull him forward and sweep your right foot into his left shin. Your pull and his loss of a supporting leg should cause him to fall to his hands and knees. When he does, move your left hand to his lower back to momentarily control him and maintain the grasp your right hand has on his lapel.

Next, throw your left leg over his back and use your left hand to seize the cloth covering his left thigh, Chivichyan says. Roll across his back and land on your left shoulder, using your left calf to pin his body against yours. Your grip on his uniform keeps him close and rotates him onto your stomach. As soon as he lands, immobilize him with your legs and pull his lapel to finish the choke. Use your grip on his pants to deny him a chance to escape.

Achilles Lock

Whether you compete with or without a uniform, the Achilles lock should be part of your arsenal, Chivichyan insists. Begin the technique by locking up with your opponent, then placing your right arm over his left shoulder so you can grab a fistful of cloth on his back. Use your left hand to grasp his right sleeve, and once you have control of the limb, immediately throw it skyward to clear a path to his body. Move forward until your chest

Achilles lock: Chivichyan grasps his opponent's sleeve and drapes his arm across his back (1). He then lifts the man's arm (2) and scoots forward as he inserts his own arm between the opponent's legs (3). After grabbing his uniform, Chivichyan lifts him (4) and drops him to the mat, where he controls the other man's limbs (5). The grappling expert then sits back and places the opponent's lower leg under his arm (6). To complete the technique, Chivichyan links his hands, leans backward and hyperextends the ankle (7).

is against his abdomen and your neck is lodged in his armpit. Snake your left arm between his legs and grab his trousers in the back, then hoist him into the air before slamming him to the mat.

Once he hits, wrap your left arm around his trapped leg and your right

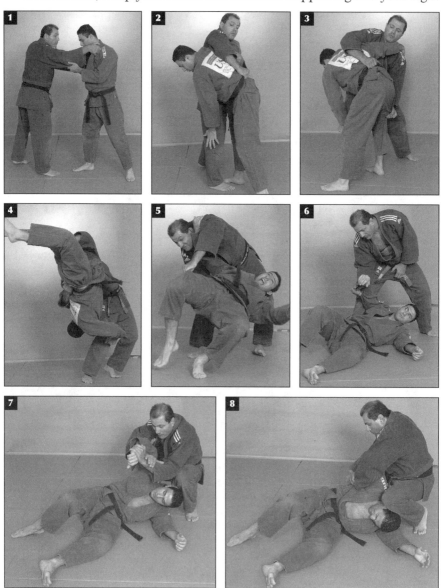

Key-lock shoulder crank: Chivichyan and his opponent grab each other's uniform (1). Chivichyan yanks the man toward him and reaches over his shoulder to grab his belt (2). He then lifts him (3-4) and slams him down (5). Chivichyan quickly takes control of the man's wrist (6), then squats and key-locks the limb (7). He finishes by pushing the opponent's head down and twisting his arm clockwise (8).

146

arm around his trapped arm. Fall to the mat and pin his calf under your left arm. Release your hold on his arm and link that hand with your left to perform an Achilles lock. The hold works by hyperextending his ankle and applying pressure to the tendon located just above his heel. Your legs prevent him from escaping as you lean backward and lift your hips to maximize your force.

Key-Lock Shoulder Crank

Start by holding your opponent's left lapel and right sleeve, Chivichyan says. Pull him forward and lean to your left to make it easier to thrust your right arm over his shoulder and across his back to catch his belt. Position your body close to his so you can leverage him into the air and slam him to the mat.

When he hits, immediately seize his right wrist with your left hand. Crouch next to his neck and shoulder, then key-lock his bent limb. To finish, place your left knee on the side of his head and torque his trapped arm clockwise to exert pressure on his shoulder.

Armbar Submission

Square off with your opponent and close the distance until you can grab his left sleeve at the cuff and shoulder. Lean backward and lift as a feint, Chivichyan says. As he resists, dart forward, place your right arm around his back and grasp the side of his uniform jacket. Muscle his left arm down between his legs while you drop to one knee and flip his body over your rolling torso.

Once he lands on his back, pin his arm against your chest and shift your legs until you can position your right one across his left thigh. At the same time, trap his left hand under your left arm and use your chest to hyperextend his elbow for the submission.

Technique Is Not Enough

Chivichyan cautions all his students that mastering a handful of grappling techniques will not necessarily guarantee victory in the ring. Likewise, strength—even when coupled with technique—is not a surefire ticket to the top.

"It doesn't matter how tough you are," says Chivichyan, who was *Black Belt's* 1997 Judo Instructor of the Year. "You can be the best technical guy in the world, but if you don't have endurance, when you're tired everything goes out the window."

His secret to building stamina depends on what you hope to do with yourself. "If you're preparing for no-holds-barred fighting, that's what you should do all the time," he says. "If you're only going to fight in judo matches, you have to train hard under judo rules. When you get tired, you should take a short break, then continue. That's the only way to develop real endurance that's specific to your type of fighting—and the only way to win."

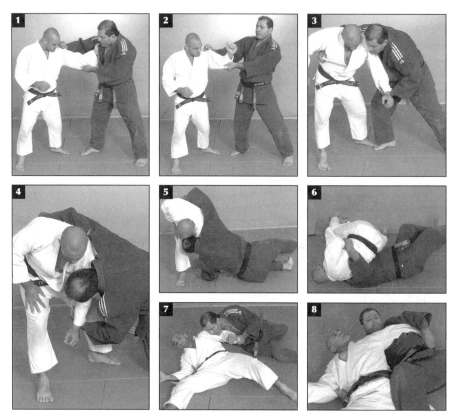

Armbar submission: Chivichyan grabs his opponent's arm (1). He leans backward and pulls to get him to react (2), then moves forward, reaches around his back and grabs his uniform (3). While forcing the man's arm downward (4), Chivichyan drops his body (5) and flips him (6). As soon as the opponent lands, the grappler adjusts his position (7) to hold him down while he hyperextends his elbow (8).

THE NECK
How to Use the Grappler's Secret Weapon and How to Strengthen the Muscles That Support It!

by Andrew Zerling • Photos by Tiago Molinos • October 2004

A thick neck sends out a warning: The person is probably strong, and he may well be a trained grappler.

That cautionary message is clear to martial artists because they know the body part can be a powerful weapon, especially when it's coupled with the right technical knowledge. Furthermore, because the neck is often a target for strikes, chokes and cranks, a developed one announces that the person standing under it is willing and able to absorb punishment.

Anatomically, the neck is the pillar that supports the head, but for ground fighters, it also has the capability of functioning as a third arm. When developed properly, it can help them nullify their opponent's techniques while implementing their own attacks. Because any chain is only as strong as its weakest link, neck work needs to be incorporated into every martial artist's training—including yours.

The neck plays an important role while defending against the front triangle choke. Andrew Zerling (top) frames his arms on Renzo Gracie's lower stomach and arches his body before Gracie can lock his legs for the submission. Powerful support muscles are required because the pressure on the neck is so great.

Offense

Because most fights start while the participants are on their feet, a discussion about the neck logically begins with takedowns. If you know how to wrestle, chances are single- and double-leg takedowns are an essential component of your arsenal. During the execution of those moves, your power begins in your lower body and ends at your head. Your neck channels the energy from the rest of your body, allowing your head and neck to enhance your ability to perform the takedowns, says Brazilian-*jujutsu* expert Renzo Gracie.

If you attempt a single- or double-leg maneuver, your opponent may counter by sprawling or shooting his legs backward and positioning his upper body on top of yours. The part of your body that bears the brunt of his action will probably be your neck because as you scramble for a better position, his torso will be resting on the back of your head. To prevail, you must be able to endure the weight long enough to slip into a better position.

Various chokes and arm locks also depend on the neck for success. Among them are the rear-naked choke and side-naked choke, both of which are enhanced when you use your head and neck to apply pressure against

Gracie executes a rear-naked choke on Zerling. To make the technique tighter and minimize the possibility of being counterattacked, Gracie uses his neck to exert additional pressure.

From the mount, Gracie feeds his opponent's collar into his right hand (1), then grips it deep (2). Next, he swings his left arm over the man's head (3) and crosses his limbs to perform a cross-gi blood choke (4). To keep from being rolled off, Gracie "bases out" with his head and neck, creating a stable tripodlike base (5).

your opponent's head. In *Mastering Jujitsu*, Gracie and co-author John Danaher note how the head assists in the execution of the rear choke: The head and the forearms become opposing forces that act on the adversary's neck to complete the hold.

For some arm locks, the head and neck function as a vise or an extra arm to hold your opponent's limb in place. When subduing a particularly tenacious foe, you may need to use your whole body to get the job done, and that's when a strong neck can be the deciding factor.

Whether you're standing or on the mat, any time you're chest to chest with your opponent and unable to engage your arms, a head butt can be just what the doctor ordered. Obviously, a strong neck is required if you hope to slam your skull into a target and recover quickly enough to take advantage of the situation. Remember that such a strike will not always end the fight, but it will definitely create an opening for a submission hold or knockout blow.

Defense

Studying the grappling arts forces you to practice seemingly endless breakfalls. The higher and more forceful the fall, the more important your neck muscles become. Tightly tucking your chin to your chest keeps the impact from whipping your head back when you land. *Aikido* master Yukio Utada once said that his years of breakfall training had probably increased his collar size.

As a grappler, you must remain aware of your balance and base. When you have an advantageous top position—such as the mount, the knee-on-the-stomach position or the side control—your stability can be used to negate the actions of a thrashing opponent. At times, you may have to preserve your positional advantage by placing your head or neck on the ground like an extra arm. Called "basing out," the maneuver can prevent you from being rolled over long enough to reorient yourself or work for a submission. Brazilian jujutsu includes scores of submission holds and escapes that exploit the ability to base out with your head, Gracie says.

The need for neck conditioning becomes obvious the first time you attempt to fight off a choke or crank. Being able to dish out punishment is important, but being able to take it can be even more critical. To win, you must first survive.

In striking, a powerful neck can save the day. Whenever a punch connects with your head, the muscles of your neck act as a shock absorber, writes Dr. Joseph Estwanik in *Sports Medicine for the Combat Arts*. Being able to absorb such blows is particularly beneficial when you're facing a skilled striker because he'll probably be a headhunter. Of course, your preferred response will involve evasion or blocking, but when all else fails, you'll want to be able to weather any punches that connect with your head.

Conditioning

Engaging in grappling practice and competition on a regular basis will certainly whip your neck muscles into shape. Adding gym training can get you to your goal even more quickly. Because of the delicate nature of

Beginning from the knee-on-the-stomach position, Gracie grabs his opponent's collar in preparation for what looks like a choke (1). The Brazilian-jujutsu instructor then grips the collar with his right hand (2) and maneuvers his left arm over the man's head, prompting the opponent to seize his collar to stop the technique (3). Gracie counters by securing the elbow of the extended limb with his head, neck and arm (4). To finish, he uses his free arm to apply pressure on the trapped elbow (5).

the spinal column, always consult a physician before starting an exercise program that works your neck.

The neck moves in six directions—forward (to place your chin on your chest), backward (to look at the ceiling), to either side (called "ear to shoulder"), and twisting to the left and right. The action of circling your neck combines all of the motions and, therefore, is a valuable stretching method. Work your neck daily to increase its flexibility and lower the risk of injury. Perform all movements slowly and properly.

Strengthening the support structure of your neck is also important.

According to Estwanik, in addition to isometrics—which can be done alone or with a partner—machines such as those manufactured by Nautilus are effective for developing the relevant muscles. One such device is the four-way neck machine, in which you place your head against a padded rest. It allows you to move forward, backward and to the sides. Another, called the rotary neck machine, permits you to twist your head against resistance.

You can also use a head harness with suspended weights, which allows you to perform forward, backward and side-to-side movements. No matter which method you select, start with light resistance and gradually increase it. Be prepared for minor after-workout stiffness because in everyday life, you don't exert your neck muscles much, and they probably won't be used to the added load.

If you've done any wrestling, you may be wondering where the wrestler's bridge fits into the equation. After all, it's a staple of most high-school programs. Here's the scoop: The wrestler's bridge is an advanced neck exercise in which only your head and feet support your body, and it can be dangerous if done improperly. If you really want to add it to your routine, seek out personalized instruction from a qualified wrestling coach or other expert. Estwanik summed it up nicely when he wrote: "Bridging as an exercise must be practiced in respectful moderation. View [it] as a technique to be learned, not as a safe repetitive exercise."

Necking Time

The first step in improving as a martial artist is recognizing the role various body parts play in the execution of your techniques. Now that you've learned how your neck can assist you offensively and defensively, all that's left is the training. Do it diligently, and in short order you'll be enjoying all the benefits a strong and conditioned neck has to offer. Then, if you find yourself up against a seasoned grappler and it feels like you're fighting an octopus, at least you'll have a third arm to rely on.

UP FOR GRABS!
Effective Judo Strategies for the Mat and the Street

by Sara Fogan and Robert W. Young • Photos by Rick Hustead • May 2005

In the early days of judo, practitioners would challenge *jujutsu* stylists to all-out fights to prove which art was superior. Because weight classes were unheard of, there ended up being a lot of small guys fighting a lot of big guys. Judo had to function as a David-vs.-Goliath art if it was to survive. Its adherents quickly discovered that if they had speed and technique, they could nullify their opponent's strength advantage.

So says Mike Swain, an internationally known judo practitioner who won a bronze medal at the 1988 Seoul Olympics. He insists that same mix of speed and technique is just as potent on the mat today, but if you ever need to employ the grappling and throwing art on the street, you may need to spice it up a bit—by avoiding certain techniques and sprinkling in some striking. The following are his favorite fighting philosophies for turning the tables on your opponent no matter where the action takes place.

Control His Body

In a judo tournament, if you throw your opponent onto his back with force and control, you'll earn a full point and win the match. "It's like a knockout," the *Black Belt* Hall of Fame member says. A similar logic applies to the street because when a person is hurled to the pavement, chances are he'll be incapacitated.

If the throw doesn't work quite right and your adversary falls on his side or his hands and knees, you must use your weight to control him, Swain says. "If you give him any space, he can escape."

If you happen to be on the wrong end of a throw, once you're on the ground you should keep your elbows and knees tucked in, he says. "I call it the 'beach-ball theory.' If you jump on a beach ball, you roll off. If an opponent tries to smother you with his body, you can grab him and roll him off you."

This posture is also useful in self-defense because it protects your vital areas. You don't want to leave your legs open because your groin will be exposed, and you don't want your body to be spread out because your torso will be vulnerable, he says. Plus, the defensive position makes it more difficult for your foe to climb on top and immobilize you.

Triangle choke from the top: Mike Swain controls his opponent by holding his shoulder and belt (1). He places his right heel behind the man's left triceps so he can't pull back into the turtle position, then puts his left knee on the ground close to his heel to form a triangle with the opponent's head and arm trapped (2). Swain then uses his weight to turn the man onto his side and simultaneously secures his left arm by pulling it across his body (3). With his legs effecting the triangle choke, the judo expert grabs the man's uniform or belt (4) to secure his right arm (5).

Feel Your Way

Whether you're rolling in the Olympics or fighting for your survival, your consciousness must be uncluttered so you can sense your opponent's movements, Swain says. Once you've freed it of extraneous thoughts, you'll be better able to expect the unexpected—and react to it.

When you're in grappling range, your awareness should be more about feeling what your enemy is doing than about seeing him move, he says. He likens this principle to dancing: Instead of looking at your partner's feet to determine where she's going, look directly in her eyes. Judo requires that a slight adjustment be made: Divert your gaze to your opponent's chest and use your peripheral vision to keep track of what's going on around you.

A valuable exercise entails practicing *randori* (free sparring) with a partner after both of you have donned a blindfold. "Let your body feel which way your opponent is going to move," Swain says. "When you have a dance partner, you have to know when to step [to avoid crushing] her toes. It's the same with judo: You have to *feel* when [your opponent] is off-balance."

Break His Balance

Disrupting your opponent's balance is the key to executing nearly every judo throw, says the San Jose, California-based instructor. In competition, you're restricted to using legal judo moves to destabilize him, but on the street, you're free to use strikes or even dirty tricks to catch him off-guard and set him up for a finishing technique.

A sleeve grip is the most important grip in tournaments because it also helps you get in the right position to execute a throw, Swain says. While that move can work on an opponent who's wearing a sturdy shirt or a jacket, it won't function against a T-shirt. Fortunately, it's not as serious a problem as it was in the past.

"A lot of the techniques that are done in Olympic competition today don't rely on a *gi*," Swain says. "They rely on wrist grabs and leg kicks. There's a lot more wrestling influence these days. It comes from the European side of judo, like with the Russians and their *sambo.*"

Arm lock from the side mount: Swain positions his chest across his opponent's chest for control and applies a figure-4 lock on his far arm (1). To exert pressure, he lifts his right elbow while keeping his left elbow on the ground (2).

Action and Reaction

Many *judoka* have a favorite throw they'll use whenever the opportunity presents itself. Contrary to what some instructors claim, that's not necessarily a bad thing, Swain says. In fact, it can make all the moves in their arsenal more effective by intimidating their opponent. And because they've probably practiced the technique to perfection, it ought to serve as a devastating method of self-defense.

"If the person you're facing fears your favorite throw, your other techniques, like the backward throw and foot sweeps, work better because your

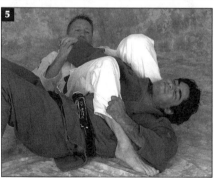

Collar-choke turnover with optional armbar: From the side position, Swain grabs his adversary's belt and far lapel (1). He then steps over the man's back with his right leg and tightens the hold on his neck (2). Next, the judoka rolls over the opponent and uses his right leg to take the man with him (3). Once the roll is completed, Swain uses his left knee to push against the man's neck while he pulls with his left hand (4). If necessary, the judo expert can transition into an armbar (5).

opponent reacts to you coming in for your favorite throw," he says.

Sometimes your opponent will employ as a counter the same technique you're using—which is often the case with the *osotogari*, or outer-reaping throw. "What makes a throw work is the courage to attack with your entire body," Swain says. "You can't just come in halfway because that's when you get countered."

Take It to the Street

Virtually any judo technique that works in competition will work on the street, Swain says. In addition to the technical knowledge you have—and which your opponent probably doesn't—you'll have an advantage because you're used to employing force against force in grappling range. Just as important, you'll know how to fall without hurting yourself.

If you determine there's a need for it, you can always throw a punch or kick to set up a judo technique or to finish one. "In competition, you'd have to use the person's uniform to pull him off-balance," Swain says. "On the street, you can just strike him and he'll be off-balance. Then you can follow through with your throw."

Your follow-through can include just about any judo move you like with the exception of the hip throw, he says. That's because in a street fight, the last thing you should do is turn your back to your opponent, even if it's for an instant.

The most effective moves in such a post-strike situation are sweeps and rear-leg trips, he says. "When someone's grabbing you and pushing you, he'll usually have one leg forward. You can take that leg out with your foot, and it'll happen so quickly that he can't even see it."

Head-and-arm side choke: As the opponent closes the gap, Swain traps his head and arm and pulls him in close (1). He then pushes the arm down and against the side of his neck while maneuvering out from under him (2). To finish, Swain sits up while pulling the man's collar and controlling his hips (3).

Extreme Techniques

As soon as your opponent falls, you should keep him down while you try to turn him over and control him or lock his arm, Swain says. Alternatively, you can shoot for a choke. Usually executed from behind, judo chokes are so effective because they cut off the blood supply to the brain, causing the person to pass out in seconds.

If you'd rather not mess with unconsciousness, go for a standing arm lock. Although it's no longer permitted in judo competition, he says, it's still a great self-defense tool that can hyperextend a limb and incapacitate an assailant.

The technique is executed as follows: When the aggressor punches, grab the wrist of his attacking arm and pull it forward. Then press your chest against his elbow and put all your weight on the joint, Swain says. At that point, he has two options: to hit the floor face-first or allow his arm to snap. Neither one will be pretty.

SUBMISSION GRAPPLING VS. CLASSICAL JUJUTSU
When Cultures and Concepts Collide

by Stephan Kesting and Alexander Kask • Photos courtesy of Stephan Kesting and Alexander Kask • May 2005

There are many similarities between submission grappling and classical Japanese *jujutsu*. Both emphasize grappling over striking. Both recognize the importance and efficiency of ground fighting. Both employ chokes, arm locks, leg locks and other submission holds.

Despite these similarities, however, there are profound differences between the old art and the new sport, including strategies, techniques and training methods. This article will examine both systems to discover where the similarities lie, why differences have emerged and what martial artists can learn from it all.

Submission Grappling

A new sport with a long history, submission grappling has as its objective the scoring of points and/or the submission of the opponent. To accomplish that, practitioners use a variety of joint locks and chokes. They usually opt not to wear a *gi*, which increases the amount of speed and athleticism required to win while limiting the options for sweeping and submission techniques.

For the most part, submission grappling is based on Brazilian jujutsu. It's a South American grappling art descended from pre-World War II judo, which was heavily influenced by the classical jujutsu systems of medieval Japan. The influence of Brazilian jujutsu on submission grappling can be seen in the types of positions and submissions commonly used in the sport.

Other grappling arts have also left their mark on submission grappling. The most common takedowns come from freestyle wrestling. Numerous leg locks come from *sambo* and catch-as-catch-can wrestling, the ancestor of pro wrestling. Many top submission grapplers also compete in mixed-martial arts or no-holds-barred events, thus bringing a higher intensity level to the sport.

Technique-wise, submission grappling is similar to what's seen in the Ultimate Fighting Championship and the PRIDE Fighting Championships, minus the strikes and kicks. Positions and maneuvers that would be advantageous in a real fight—such as passing the guard and achieving the mount—are rewarded with points.

Training in submission grappling typically involves significant amounts of sparring, or "rolling." Bouts with a resisting opponent are considered

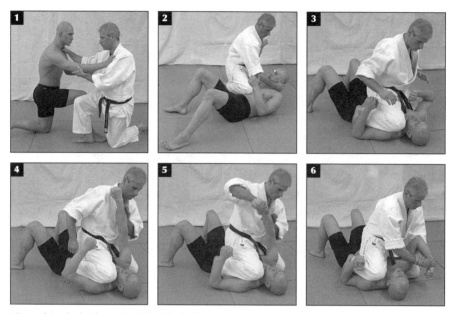

Classical arm lock: Alexander Kask (right) locks up with his opponent, seizing pressure points at the elbow and neck (1). He turns to his left to trip the man, then drops a knee onto his liver area (2). Next, Kask slides his knee up to pin his opponent's shoulder (3). When the man punches, he parries the blow with his left hand (4), then secures his wrist with his right hand (5) and applies an elbow and wrist lock (6).

crucial in the development of the skills and attributes needed for high-level performance.

Classical Jujutsu

Jujutsu is the term used to describe a number of close-quarters-combat systems developed by the samurai. Initially, it was only a supplement to techniques that employed the sword, spear and bow because unarmed combat was viewed as the last resort on the battlefield. It was called into action in melee combat when weapons were broken or rendered useless by the proximity of the opponents. Early jujutsu focused on lethal armored grappling techniques and the use of improvised weapons.

The classical jujutsu techniques that are the focus of this article come from one of the oldest systems, *takenouchi-ryu.* It was developed by a warrior named Takenouchi Hisamori during Japan's Warring States period (1467-1573). The techniques shown in the accompanying photographs are from the *bitchu-den* lineage of takenouchi-ryu, which is led by 16th-generation headmaster Ono Yotaro. It emphasizes unarmed combat skills, as well as training in the use of the long sword, short sword, dagger, long

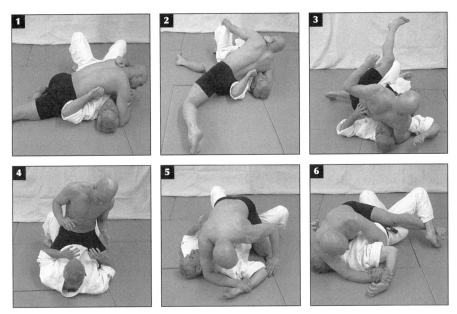

Modern arm lock: Stephan Kesting pins his opponent in a side mount (1). He switches his base and faces the man's legs while maintaining control over his upper body (2). Next, Kesting swings his left leg upward (3) and maneuvers to the mount (4). From that position, he catches the opponent's right wrist and drives it to the floor, placing his elbow beside his ear (5). He then applies a figure-4 arm lock, dragging his hand on the floor while lifting his elbow (6).

staff, and sickle and chain.

The classical jujutsu leg lock, arm lock and choking techniques illustrated here are classified as *yoroi kumiuchi,* or armored grappling. These techniques taught the samurai how to grapple while wearing armor and struggling with an opponent who's wearing armor. The emphasis is on joint locks, chokes and strikes that would have attacked portions of the body that armor didn't cover, as well as using the extra weight of the armor against the opponent.

Training in classical jujutsu is done by way of *kata.* A kata is a predetermined sequence of techniques that involves two partners (more, in some cases) in various combative scenarios. It teaches strategy while developing physical and psychological attributes. Working within prearranged routines allows the use of otherwise lethal techniques and weapons at full speed, thus keeping the incidence of injury low.

Submission Grappling vs. Classical Jujutsu

The differences between submission grappling and classical jujutsu fall into three categories: strategy, techniques and training methods. There are various historical and cultural reasons for these variances, and learning about them will expand your knowledge base no matter which pursuit you favor.

Strategic Differences

As stated above, the goal of submission grappling is to submit your opponent or defeat him on points, and the goal of classical jujutsu was to win on the battlefield, usually in the presence of weapons and multiple attackers and often while encumbered by armor. These divergent aims led to quite different strategies.

Submission grapplers and the medieval samurai had different concerns while fighting on the ground. For example, countless modern-day competitions have proved that the rear mount is a powerful way to control an opponent. It leaves him vulnerable to a number of submissions and limits his options for escape and counterattack. The position isn't favored in classical jujutsu, however, because disengaging from an opponent can be difficult to do quickly. The knee-in-the-spine control is preferred, even though it's less secure, because it can be abandoned more rapidly if a second attacker suddenly appears.

Similarly, the presence of weapons is an important strategic consideration. Classical jujutsu teaches many defenses against wrist grabs. Some modern martial artists find this emphasis strange, given that so few

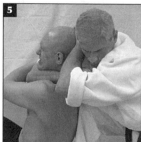

Classical choke: Kask kneels over his adversary (1). When the man tries to sit up (2), Kask places his knee against his spine and reaches around his neck (3). He then bends his arm and grasps his left biceps with his right palm (4). He finishes with the sleeper hold, ensuring that his head is turned to avoid an eye attack (5).

confrontations begin this way nowadays. In the sword culture of medieval Japan, however, wrist-grab defenses carried a sense of urgency because a person grabbing your wrist might have been trying to draw his own weapon while stopping you from drawing yours.

Differences in Technique

There are many similarities in the chokes and joint locks of submission grappling and classical jujutsu. There are, after all, only a limited number of directions in which you can bend an arm, twist a foot and constrict a neck. Nevertheless, there are important differences in how the techniques are applied.

Classical jujutsu uses some pressure-point attacks, whereas submission grappling tends to rely on structural attacks. As an illustration of this principle, consider the leg lock shown in the accompanying photos. The classical-jujutsu practitioner crushes the calf muscle and attacks a pressure point midway down the lower leg. In a similar attack, the submission grappler attacks the ankle itself, threatening to tear the ligaments, muscles and tendons that attach the foot to the lower leg.

This reliance on pressure points is a divergence between old and new. The use of pressure points in classical grappling stems from a variety of factors. In some cases, the point being targeted was in a location that wasn't protected by the armor of the era. In certain instances, the samurai used a

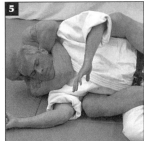

Modern choke: Kesting controls his opponent with the butterfly guard and grips his right triceps with his right hand (1). He then pulls his foe forward while moving to the left (2) and climbs onto his back (3). Once he's assumed the rear mount, Kesting snakes his right arm around the man's throat (4) and uses his legs to control him as he applies a rear-naked choke (5).

Classical leg lock: After throwing his enemy down, Kask controls him (1). The man kicks, and Kask parries his leg with a circular clockwise sweep using his right arm (2). He then wraps his arm around the leg and traps it in his armpit (3). Next, Kask grabs his own right forearm with his left hand and leans back with his knees tight against the man's leg (4). The pain is inflicted as he grinds his forearm against a pressure point in the opponent's calf (5). The encounter is terminated by a leg raise (6) and a heel kick to the groin (7).

Modern leg lock: Kesting shoots in (1) and effects a double-leg takedown (2). When his opponent lands on the mat, Kesting encircles his left ankle with his right arm and falls back, controlling the leg with his left shin and right foot (3). The Achilles lock applies pressure on the ankle just above the heel. To finish, Kesting increases the pressure by arching his back (4).

pressure-point technique to harness the pain response and create openings for subsequent submissions or strikes.

In submission grappling, ultradangerous techniques like gouging the throat or eyes are illegal in competition because of safety concerns. Furthermore, not all pressure-point attacks work against all people, including fighters who possess a high pain tolerance and can ignore the discomfort.

Another difference occurs after a successful submission has been executed. In modern grappling, the match is over. In old Japan, however, an opponent with a broken arm or dislocated leg was still considered dangerous. As a result, classical-jujutsu kata often follow a submission with additional strikes and maneuvers designed to ensure that the opponent no longer poses a threat.

The presence or absence of armor also plays a role in determining how techniques are executed. Limited mobility, protection of certain joints and body areas, and the use of an opponent's armor against him were all factors the samurai had to contend with but the modern grappler does not.

Consider the classical leg lock shown in this article: After executing it, the martial artist kicks his foot into the air to simulate moving the armored flap that protects the groin out of the way. He then drops his heel into the man's groin to finish the confrontation.

Differences in Training Methods

Ultimately, it's the differences in training methods that create the most profound divergences between the old and new approaches to combative grappling. How are the techniques actually practiced? What methods are used to develop proficiency and technical expertise? What is the training "culture"? The answers can heavily influence the development and outward form of any art.

As mentioned earlier, most classical-jujutsu training revolved around kata and the repetition of specific combat scenarios with one or more partners. This approach is very different from the rough-and-tumble training sessions of submission grapplers, where sparring is always emphasized. Classical-jujutsu proponents contend that their techniques are too lethal to practice in an unrehearsed context. Submission grapplers argue that the benefits gained from being able to spar full power far outweigh the disadvantages of being limited to less-lethal techniques.

The goals of modern practitioners are also different. Most classical-jujutsu stylists today believe that preserving their art in its original state is important, and they don't welcome changes to their kata, techniques or training methods. This is illustrated by the fact that most serious jujutsu students can trace their lineage back to a single person in medieval Japan. Submission grapplers, on the other hand, are interested in surviving and winning on the mat. If they think they've found a more efficient way to take someone down and choke him, they'll adopt it. Their sport is evolving rapidly, and techniques fall in and out of favor on an annual basis.

Finally, there's a profound difference in the way information is spread among practitioners of the two arts. Knowledge of techniques in medieval Japan was often a life-and-death matter for the samurai. Consequently, there was a strong tradition of secrecy, and each *ryu* (system) had its "closed door" techniques that were entrusted only to reliable senior students.

In the modern world, however, information can no longer be kept secret. Grapplers attend seminars and private classes. Instructional DVDs and videos of competitions are widely available. Magazines show a competitor's favorite moves. Forums on the Internet openly debate the best way to apply techniques. This represents an unprecedented development in the history of the martial arts, and it's the main reason the sport of submission grappling is growing and evolving so quickly.

Summary

The study of these two approaches to combative grappling can be fascinating and rewarding. The classical way emphasizes issues related to culture, history and the perils of total combat. Modern submission grappling, on the other hand, offers an efficient vehicle for the development of skills and tactics. It's the opinion of the authors that practitioners of each art can benefit from being exposed to the methods of the other.

GRACIE FIGHTING SECRETS REVEALED!
Marcio Feitosa Talks About Training, Techniques and Teams in Brazil

by Stephan Kesting • Photos courtesy of Stephan Kesting • July 2005

*M*arcio Feitosa is the head instructor for Gracie Barra, the Brazilian-jujutsu team headed by Carlos Gracie Jr. that has produced such competitors as Renzo Gracie, the Machado brothers, Nino Schembri and others. Experienced in competition, Feitosa counts among his victories the prestigious Abu Dhabi Combat Club Championship, the World Brazilian Jiu-Jitsu Championship and the Pan-American Championship. In this exclusive interview, he discusses the state of the grappling art in the land of its birth.

—S.K.

Black Belt: How did you get started in the martial arts?

Marcio Feitosa: I started to train with Carlos Gracie Jr. when I was 12. I grew up at the academy. My father left my family, so my brother and I took care of my mother and two sisters. Carlos knew I had to make money, and he always gave me jobs as a *jujutsu* teacher. I've earned my living from teaching jujutsu since I was 15, teaching every day. I am 28 years old and have had my black belt for nine years.

I did not get ready to be a great fighter; I got ready to become a great teacher. I prepared myself as a fighter when I had a bit of extra time. I never had two or three weeks to get ready for a tournament. I was always teaching classes, and at the end, I got ready for the tournament.

BB: Does the Gracie Barra school have a characteristic style of jujutsu?

Feitosa: I don't think so because we never train primarily for competition. At the academy, there is no incentive for students to specialize in competition because we think that when you teach this way, you limit a student's game.

For example, some academies spend all their time on guard passing and guard defense because that is where you are most of the time during competition. Or they try to find a certain talent that a kid has so they can improve it, score points and win tournaments. Our biggest goal is never to win competitions; it is to improve people's minds and spirits through jujutsu. We try to use jujutsu as a mirror for the student's life. We try to work the whole picture: the techniques, the way of life. If you limit the techniques because you are preparing only for tournaments, imagine what else you are going to leave out of that student's training.

Today, we do things in a certain way, and I'm not sure if it is the proper way to practice jujutsu. Long ago, jujutsu used to be more individual, but it used to be really expensive. Today, we have much bigger classes with 80 or 90 people, so there is no way you can let the people spar for half an hour at a time. Today, we do interval training, and usually we use 10-minute rounds. We encourage them to let the game flow, to fight from every position and to feel safe in whatever position the person is in.

In the old days, you didn't really spar in rounds. The guys used to spar once or twice, but when they sparred, they kept on going until one person tapped or asked for a rest. Carlos Gracie Jr. still trains that way today; he never does interval training. He calls a partner, and they spar for 25 or 30 minutes. If he's feeling good or if the other guy taps early, then Carlos might train twice.

BB: Does Gracie Barra emphasize *vale tudo*, or no-holds-barred fighting?

Feitosa: No. Carlos never wanted to push people to go out there and fight in no-holds-barred because you can hurt yourself bad. Vale tudo fighting was very important in jujutsu history, but Carlos didn't want anyone to take vale tudo as a way of life because he didn't take it for himself.

I did one no-rules fight, but Carlos never pushed me to do it. He said,

Marcio Feitosa (top) maneuvers into position to complete the Americana arm lock.

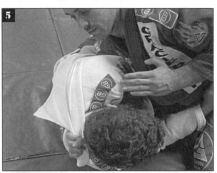

Brabo choke counter to the half-guard: Feitosa is caught in his opponent's half-guard (1). Feitosa uses his right hand to free the man's left lapel and stretch it behind his body (2) before passing it to his left hand (3). Next, he maneuvers his right arm between their bodies (4) and grasps the same lapel with his right hand (5). Feitosa then grips the lapel with his left hand and applies a nutcracker technique to the man's neck (6). The Brazilian-jujutsu expert finalizes the choke by bringing his arms together and rocking his weight forward (7).

"If you want to go, that's OK." He always showed us the techniques for vale tudo but never pushed us to specialize in it.

Then vale tudo became a big business, and a lot of our students started to ask for it. They were saying, "I want to make money from this; I want to make it my way of life." So Carlos said: "OK, you guys are asking for it. I don't want you to go out there and mess up your face." He helps with all the jujutsu techniques but doesn't want to be the figurehead of the team. Now they have a wrestling coach, a *muay Thai* coach and a manager who takes care of the team.

BB: Do you train with and without a *gi*?

Feitosa: We used to train only with a gi; nowadays, we do no-gi every Friday. But even on Fridays, at least half of our students show up with a gi. Guys like training with a gi much more than training without it. I also like a gi much better. After a while training without a gi, you don't have as much to do. It's not as technical. With a gi, you have to think much more, and it keeps your interest alive. With a gi, you can continue to improve for your whole life, and without a gi, there is not as much technique involved.

BB: Do you believe there is an "old jujutsu" and a "new jujutsu"?

Feitosa: Not really. There isn't an old and new jujutsu, but the techniques are always improving. There aren't rules that limit your moves on the ground; that's why jujutsu is amazing. People are always developing new techniques. For example, I learn a lot from my students. Even an average guy has at least one area that he is very strong at. If you pay attention to this area, you will learn something from him. This way, the technique keeps on developing.

The biggest difference that I see between the old school and the people today isn't so much about techniques like the half-guard and butterfly guard. Today, many of the clubs just focus on competition and making good fighters; they concentrate on a few techniques and conditioning. There are so many other things included in jujutsu that people are forgetting.

Before, they used to do it much better. They involved you in a way of life. They used to be good on the ground, but they also knew the complete self-defense program and the takedowns. Today, people are mutilating jujutsu. Some guys have no stand-up fighting. They come out and are almost lying down on the mats in their eagerness to jump to the guard. If they are on top, they are dead.

On the ground at a lot of gyms, people only know how to pass the guard and defend the guard. If you let a guy from the old school pin you in the side mount, you're going to tap for sure. You see, they used to train longer, so they spent much more time in the mount, the side mount and on someone's back. So today, if you don't have as much time to spend sparring, you should at least do specific training and [practice] the mount, side-mount and back positions.

BB: Does training with a gi help your ability when you compete without a gi?

Feitosa: I've never seen a person who has only trained no-gi but feels comfortable on the bottom, in the open guard, in the closed guard, on top and so on. When someone has trained his whole life without a gi, his game is different. A gi gives you a different mobility and teaches you to work at different angles that are impossible to learn just doing no-gi.

Of course, this doesn't mean that people who have only trained no-gi won't be very tough in competition. But to be really good and a complete fighter is different.

BB: Do you think *sambo*, freestyle wrestling and other grappling arts have influenced jujutsu during the past 10 years?

Feitosa: Of course, there was an influence. I saw it when the first foreigners came to Brazil. Our single-leg and double-leg takedowns used to be completely different from today because it was enough to take the other person down. So once another person showed up with a different balance and a stronger sprawl, we stopped and studied the moves and angles. That's just one example of an influence from another style.

I remember when the first guys showed up going for kneebars and this sort of stuff—I think it came from sambo. We stopped and studied the new moves. If the guys made someone tap with this, it meant the move worked.

The Gracies were always very intelligent. They never limited jujutsu. They never said, "We don't practice techniques from another system," unless those techniques didn't work or were dangerous for training partners. They always absorbed things that worked well.

BB: Are leg locks cheap techniques?

Feitosa: It's true that foot locks don't let the game flow as nice as it can flow, but they are moves just like any other moves. The only thing we tell our students not to use is anything that rotates the knee to the inside. It's not that we don't like that move; it's because it can damage your partner. With the rotation, when you feel the pain, your knee is already injured, so that is why we stopped teaching this move. We also don't teach the cervical (spine lock) because you can hurt someone really bad with it.

It's true that some people don't like leg locks, but they work. You've got to use them, so you learn to defend against them.

BB: You tend to see more leg locks in no-gi grappling.

Feitosa: Yes. It is harder to get an arm because it's so slippery—and other things, too. When you train students how to perform foot locks with a gi, you must be more technical because the other guy will grab your collar and be able to defend much better. If he does this, you can get tired trying to pull his foot all the time.

Without a gi, it's harder for the person to defend. Your foot is slippery,

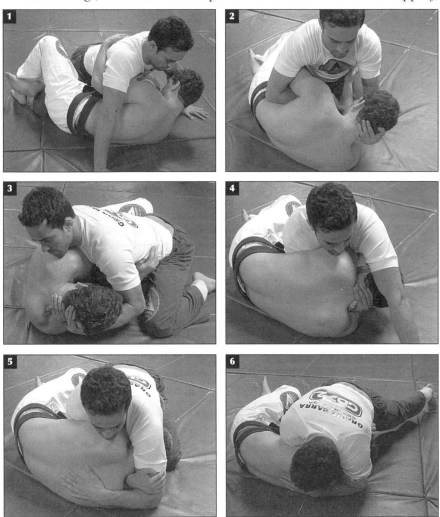

No-gi choke counter to the half-guard: Feitosa begins in his opponent's half-guard (1). He wraps his right arm around the man's left arm and uses his left hand to cup his head (2). Feitosa then inserts his right arm even more until he can cup his head with both hands (3). Next, he frees his left arm (4) and locks his right hand on his left biceps, trapping the opponent's head and arm (5). To finish the choke, he drives forward and lifts his right shoulder (6).

but once the guy catches it, it is harder to defend because you don't have a gi to hold. Also, without a gi, you have fewer submissions. You don't have the collar to use all the time, so you have fewer arm locks and chokes. So you use more foot locks, kneebars and leg locks.

BB: What advice would you give to a person who had only two months to prepare for a big competition?

Feitosa: I cannot give you a program that I would give to everyone. It depends on his game. A teacher has to have the eye to understand what is going on with his student's mind, and that is what makes it hard to be a teacher. If you figure out why a student isn't doing well in competition, you can change that. Sometimes, just through conversation, you can make someone a champion.

One guy might need a strong conditioning program because technically inferior fighters are beating him. Another guy might already be very strong but not very technical—say he isn't very good on his feet—then you want to have him do a lot of stand-up training so at least he feels a little bit safer and more confident there.

You might have a good training routine worked out, but listen to your body. If you didn't sleep well this week, you can't do as much as you did last week. The first part of training is sleeping. If you don't sleep, you can't do anything unless you are using chemicals and steroids. Steroids will let you train hard without enough sleep, but in 10 or 20 years' time, your body will complain.

BB: What are your plans for the future?

Feitosa: I've been a fighter and I've been a teacher, and I have been involved in jujutsu for a very long time. Carlos has told me: "You've got to do something better than me. You came after me, and I tried to tell you everything. Now take these things and do something."

Our plan is for me to go somewhere other than Rio and open a gym. I have many ideas I think would work so well for a jujutsu academy. Right now, we teach in a really traditional *dojo*. There are black belts who have had their belt longer than I have been alive: 28 years. So sometimes it is hard to make even the smallest change in our dojo. You have to have meetings with all these people, talk to the senior students and make them understand that times are changing. Nowadays, you need to train no-gi once in a while, have a different warm-up and so on. There are a lot of good ideas I cannot practice at the dojo I teach at.

BB: Where are you going to do this?

Feitosa: We don't have any plans yet. When we go ahead with this, we have to make sure all the instructors share the same mentality. It is easy to train someone to teach the techniques, but there are certain things I learned from Carlos and from other great guys who have been doing jujutsu for a long time but are teaching out of the country now. So I got to make sure I spread the mentality—for instance, almost none of the guys who came after me uses drugs.

There are a lot of schools where the teacher hangs out with the students, drinking and maybe even smoking drugs. We don't do these things. When the boys see me, sometimes they are even too embarrassed to drink alcohol. I drink sometimes—on the weekend I have fun with my girlfriend—but I don't drink with my students, especially with the teenagers. I am trying to be for them as Carlos was for me.

Kimura arm-lock counter to the half-guard: Feitosa lies in his opponent's half-guard (1). Feitosa encircles the man's left arm with his left arm and stabilizes himself by pushing against his knee (2). The Brazilian-jujutsu fighter then forms a figure-4 with his right hand locked onto the opponent's left wrist (3). Next, he twists his body until he's facing the floor and the trapped wrist is pinned to the mat (4). To effect the kimura, he steps over the man's head with his left leg and lifts the locked limb (5).

MASTER GRAPPLER
Brazilian-Jujutsu Pioneer Alvaro Barreto Speaks Out About the History and Techniques of His Art
Photos by Rick Hustead • October 2005

Although Brazil has no doubt produced a plethora of families that can rightly be categorized as legends in jujutsu, most American martial artists know only two: Gracie and Machado. Add the Barreto surname to that list. Alvaro Barreto is an eighth-degree black belt who took up the grappling art at age 10 under the tutelage of Helio and Carlos Gracie. At 16, he started teaching at Academie Gracie in Rio de Janeiro. In the 48 years that followed, he's trained some of the most accomplished practitioners in the art, including Sylvio Behring, Pedro Carvalho and Pedro Sauer. His brother, Joao Alberto Barreto, is also a respected master in Brazil. In this article, Alvaro Barreto talks about the art's early days, its growing pains and its current condition in Brazil and America.

—Editor

On his beginnings: I've been training in *jujutsu* full time since I was 10 years old. I fought in Rio de Janeiro with the Gracie family and my brother, Joao Alberto Barreto. Through him, I got to meet the Gracie family. Later on, when I was 16, I became one of the instructors at Academie Gracie. I taught kids. At 18, I left the academy. Then I taught classes at the academy of professor Helio Vigio. Later on, my brother left Academie Gracie to open his own business, and I went to work with him. After 10 years with my brother, I opened my own place, called Corpo Quatro Academy. I still have that academy today. It's been operating for more than 30 years.

On jujutsu students in Brazil: At my academy, I have about 150 students. But I'm also a professor at Federal University of Rio de Janeiro, so I devote much of my time to the university as well as to private classes. At my academy, classes last about an hour to an hour and a half. Normally, the adults practice every day, Monday to Friday. The children, until they're 9 years old, usually work out two times a week. For 10- to 14-year-olds, it's three times a week. I have 15 black belts under me. The whole time I've been a black belt, I've promoted only 15. I'm very strict.

On his system: My vision of jujutsu is oriented toward education and not so much toward competition, even though I've participated in a lot in

Self-defense: Alvaro Barreto (right) is held in a head lock (1). He immediately turns his body so he can place his right pinkie under the nose of his assailant (2), then uses both hands to rotate the man's body (3) into position for a guillotine choke (4).

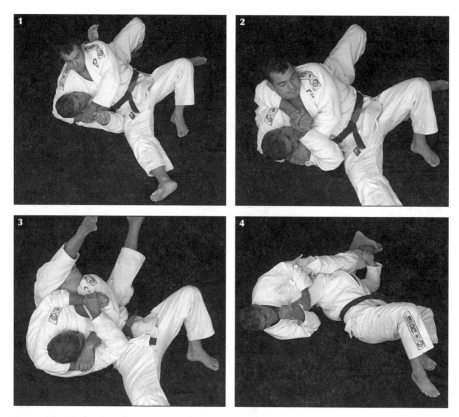

Competition: Pedro Carvalho (top) wraps his arm around the neck of Barreto (1). Barreto uses his right arm to push his left forearm upward against the neck of his opponent (2). Next, he places his left leg over the opponent's head and forces him backward (3). Once the head lock is broken, Barreto scissors his legs around the man's neck while immobilizing his right arm (4).

tournaments. I was part of building the Federation of Jiu-Jitsu, where I helped make the belt-ranking progression. If you do jujutsu every day, it takes a *minimum* of five years to reach black belt. The progression goes from white to blue to purple to brown to black for master and red for grandmaster. For children, it's white to yellow to orange to green and then blue and so on. For kids to go from white to blue belt, it's usually 25 hours for each stripe. In America, the requirements for rank need to be more rigorous, and promotions should be more monitored.

On the proper curriculum: In my vision, jujutsu is composed of four courses: self-defense, traumatic moves (locks and chokes), judo and ground fighting. To be a complete martial artist, you need to know all four because one helps the other. They're all linked. Self-defense, for example, goes onto the floor, and from there you can go into other positions. In jujutsu, competition is a consequence of education. The education gives you discipline and self-confidence. It turns you into a better citizen. I'd say there's not only an educational part but also a therapeutic part. Some people come to us and say they can't go to school because they're scared. Through jujutsu, especially the psychological aspect that teaches self-confidence, training makes them a different person. It makes them more secure.

On jujutsu's popularity: Compared to soccer, it's not very popular. But compared to other martial arts, it's now the most prevalent style in Brazil.

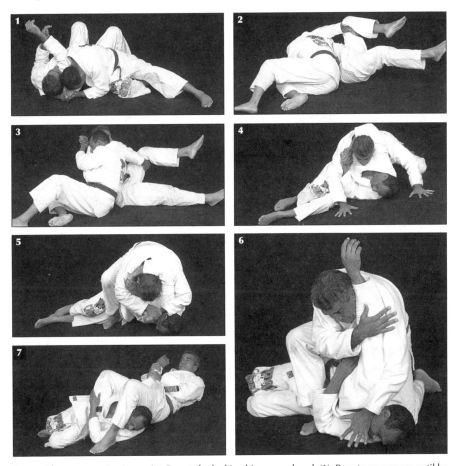

Escape: The opponent (top) restrains Barreto by locking his arm and neck (1). Barreto maneuvers until he can grasp his left leg with his right hand (2). He then leverages himself upright (3) and on top of his foe (4). Barreto uses his forearm to break the head lock (5) and takes control of the man's arm (6). To finish, he lies back and effects an armbar (7).

Choke defense: An opponent (left) attempts a collar choke on Barreto, causing Barreto to position his right arm over the man's arms (1). He places his right leg in front of the man's right leg and pivots (2), then throws him to the mat (3). Because Barreto has maintained control of the man's right arm, he can transition into one of several finishing holds.

Because it grew so fast, it's been a little disorganized. And there have been unprepared teachers. It's similar in the United States. You need an institution that brings all the students and gyms together. I'm not saying it's perfect in Brazil, because it's not. The competitions are organized, but everything else is kind of loose. Some teachers don't live correctly. A teacher should be a good citizen with a good educational background, such as from a university. That makes him better at passing on information. Students need leaders they can look up to because the majority of the time, they look for instructors to give them confidence and keep them strong.

On adding jujutsu to other arts: In the United States, many people who do jujutsu want to incorporate it into other styles. That's fine because they already have the discipline it takes to be a martial artist, so they have an advantage. The majority of the time, they abandon everything they had learned and end up doing only jujutsu.

On competition: At tournaments, referees sometimes have difficulties interpreting the rules in an ethical way. They have personal issues that can affect the outcome of matches, and that causes problems. Another problem is that there are a lot of tournaments organized by different teachers, and each one is free to make up his own rules or modify existing rules.

On his training: I'm 64, and I do everything the same way my students do. I want to stay in shape to pass on classic Brazilian jujutsu to people who have a serious mind-set for the work it involves—people like Pedro Carvalho, Pedro Sauer and my students back in Brazil. It's very important to transmit the skills we know, as well as the principles and essence of the art. That's one of the most important things I've learned. Jujutsu doesn't stop at the competition arena. Its purpose is to form not better fighters but better human beings.

DOWN AND OUT!
A Martial Artist's Guide to Wrestling's Single- and Double-Leg Attacks

by Mark Mireles • Photos by Rick Hustead • December 2005

When martial artists think of wrestling, a variety of images may come to mind: The 2000 Olympic Games, in which American underdog Rulon Gardner defeated a Russian legend for the gold; the teen flick *Vision Quest*, in which high-school wrestlers endured grueling workouts and epic duels, the junior-high gymnasium, where jocks in singlets ruled the mats.

No matter what your memories are, the common thread is undoubtedly athletic activity—even wrestlers refer to their pursuit as "man's oldest sport." Because it uses a point-based scoring system and operates under specific rules, martial artists tend to view wrestling as nothing more than a contact sport with virtually no combat application. That perspective has merit—especially when you consider there are no rules, referees or time limits in real fights—but it's far from being the last word on wrestling.

Combat sports are rampant in Western society. In addition to wrestling, we have boxing, fencing, *taekwondo*, judo, *sambo* and so on. Despite what naysayers might claim, they all offer numerous techniques that can be applied to self-defense situations. For example, the punches of boxing have been used for centuries in bar brawls and street fights for one simple reason: They're effective in hand-to-hand combat. Wrestling is no different. Throughout history, its techniques have been used in real fights because they work. In fact, renowned warrior cultures such as those fostered by the Greeks and Romans relied on wrestling to prepare their soldiers for battle.

This article will explain how the age-old grappling style can improve your effectiveness as a martial artist. It will focus on two techniques you absolutely need to know: the double-leg attack and single-leg attack. They're effective transitioning techniques, and the skilled execution of either one can alter the outcome of any fight. But before beginning, it's necessary to review the basics.

Stance

The typical wrestler's stance is good for wrestling—and for getting punched in the face or kicked in the groin. When examined through the eyes of a martial artist, numerous problems become apparent.

Therefore, a functional combat stance—one that allows you to attack with punches, kicks, clinches and takedowns, as well as defend against them—needs to be devised. It's important because in a fight, you must be in a good position at all times, and good positioning starts with a stance that's natural and fluid, not rigid and predictable. For great examples, watch any mixed-martial arts event.

You can build your own combat stance by positioning your head upright, keeping your back straight and tucking your chin near your lead shoulder. Your hands should be positioned high, just like a boxer's guard. Your forward leg should be pointed at your opponent, your rear heel should be lifted and your knees should be bent slightly. This will enable you to make your motions smooth instead of robotic.

The Setup

Five components come into play when leg attacks are used: setup, level change, penetration, collecting the knee(s) and finishing. The setup is designed to function as a pre-emptive move to distract your opponent. It entails attacking upstairs (the head) before going downstairs (the legs). In the sport of wrestling, which forbids strikes, this is accomplished by snapping the opponent's head or tapping his forehead. In MMA fighting and self-defense, however, there are few or no rules, which means that a jab to the nose or chin, a head butt or a fingertip strike to the eyes can be used. Your goal is to disrupt his line of sight or attention, if only for a split second, to buy time for the level change and penetration.

During the setup phase, proper distancing is essential. Before you

A combat stance should enable you to employ offensive moves from wrestling, boxing and the Asian martial arts, as well as counters to the most common attacks. In this example, the power leg is in the rear, and the knees are flexed for rapid deployment of a leg attack.

dart in for the takedown, you must be no farther than an arm's length away from your opponent. That's why punching is not only a good setup but also a great way to measure range. The rule is, If you can touch him, you can take him down. Conversely, if you can't reach him, your leg attack is more likely to fail because he'll have time to counter it.

Level Change and Penetration

After you execute the setup, it's time to get to work on those legs. The key involves initiating two separate but related actions: level change and penetration.

Level change refers to the act of getting below your opponent. The easiest way to accomplish that is to simply lower your body by bending your knees. For maximum effectiveness, keep your back straight and your head up.

Penetration refers to the act of exploding through your opponent. It occurs almost simultaneously with the level change. Drive off your rear foot directly toward the target using a drop-step. The drop-step involves taking a deep step, with your forward knee moving between your opponent's legs (for the double-leg attack) or to the outside of his leg (single-leg attack).

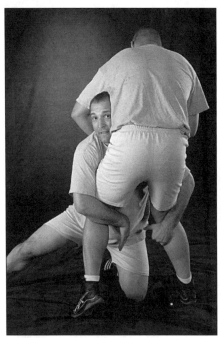

When the "big hooks" are used to control the knees, the muscles of the arms and back are pitted against the muscles of the opponent's legs.

Ideally, you should not let your knees touch the ground for two reasons: Fights often take place on hard surfaces, which can injure your knees; and anytime your knees touch the ground, the power you'll be able to direct at your opponent will decrease. In reality, though, especially with a deep level change and explosive penetration, your forward knee may come into contact with the ground. When it does, your goal should be to quickly get up and redirect your energy into the attack.

In totality, the setup, level change and penetration (with drop-step) are referred to as "a shot" or "shooting."

Double-Leg

The double-leg attack is a directed shot to both your opponent's legs simultaneously. Because of its aggressive nature, it can resemble a football tackle, but there's an important technical difference: You want your opponent to be standing with his feet in a square stance. You can't force him to orient himself this way, but you can train yourself to identify it as soon as it happens and exploit it immediately.

The double-leg continues with your forward knee and foot passing between his legs off your execution of the drop-step. Your rear leg drives you forward like a sprinter coming off the blocks. "Collecting" his knees using your limbs is of paramount importance. To better understand this phase, two terms must be introduced: "big hooks" and "little hooks."

Big hooks are the crooks of your elbows. Little hooks are your hands with your fingers pressed together and each thumb tight against its corresponding index finger, all of which are bent so your hands resemble hooks.

The large muscle groups of your opponent's legs are stronger than your arms. To overcome this disadvantage, you must attack his legs at their weakest point: the knees. Because the knees bend naturally, they're an ideal target as long as you can get your big hooks deep around them. Whenever possible, don't try to collect his knees with your little hooks. With deep penetration, you should be able sink in your big hooks and use the muscles of your arms and back.

During the execution of the double-leg attack, your head and back should be straight. Recall that the level change occurs when you bend your knees. Aim your forehead toward his solar plexus and keep it that way during the penetration. On contact, slide your head to the side of his body that's opposite your forward leg. Your shoulder should be deep in his gut. For example, if your right leg penetrates, the left side of your head and your left shoulder will make contact with his torso.

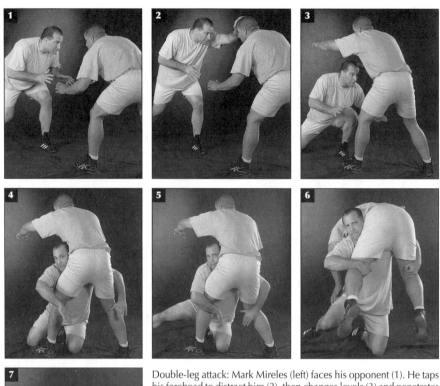

Double-leg attack: Mark Mireles (left) faces his opponent (1). He taps his forehead to distract him (2), then changes levels (3) and penetrates (4). Next, Mireles uses his "big hooks" to collect the opponent's knees, all while keeping his head up and his back straight (5). The wrestler finishes by lifting the man off his feet (6) and dropping him on the mat (7).

Two finishes are possible: the drive-through and the lift-and-dump. The drive-through is a scientific tackle. You explode into your opponent with your big hooks around his knees. When you execute the double-leg, you must hit him like a freight train to get in deep enough to finish. As you pull his knees together and into your chest, your mass keeps moving forward. Drive off the shot and push him backward with your shoulder until he falls.

The lift-and-dump is executed when you shoot in deep but your opponent doesn't fall. Instead, for a split second you're under him and

THE ULTIMATE GUIDE TO GRAPPLING

he's slightly bent over at the waist. You lift him, then drop him to the side opposite your head. The key is to explode upward, picking him up like a sack of potatoes. Be sure to keep your big hooks in place as you pull his knees in and push your ear against his rib cage. He'll drop off your shoulder and land on his back.

Single-Leg

The single-leg attack is as offensively effective as the double-leg and an excellent counter to the low-line roundhouse and midlevel front kick. Technically, it's similar to the double-leg. Although it comes in several variations, there are two you should master: the snatch and the direct.

The snatch single-leg attack starts with a quick level change, followed by grabbing the opponent's leg at the knee. It's an ideal technique to use at close range. A quick assessment of your opponent's positioning will help you determine whether the move is a viable option. You want to target the lead leg in a way that enables you to grab it with both hands. Once you change levels, extend your arms beyond his knee and secure it. It's best to use a no-thumbs grip so your digits don't get in the way when transitioning grips.

The no-thumbs gripping method is simple. As your arms meet at a 90-degree angle, place your palms together, one on top of the other, as if you're clapping. Your thumbs are aligned with your index fingers in a natural position. The arm that goes around the outside of your opponent's leg will have its palm facing down.

Once you've grabbed the knee, pull it between your thighs and grip it with your legs. Keep your back erect and ensure that your head is placed against his upper rib cage.

The direct single-leg attack starts with a good stance, followed by a level change and penetration/drop-step. However, when you shoot, your leg goes to the outside of your opponent's leg. Your arms extend beyond his knee and grip it as described above. Your head stays upright and spears into his ribs. If you manage to keep your knee(s) off the ground, you'll be in an excellent position to pull his leg between yours and trap it as you did during the snatch. But in the real world, your knee(s) will probably touch, and if that's the case, you must get up quickly. If both your knees are on the ground for a split second, it's paramount that your outside leg comes up before your inside leg.

There are many ways to finish the single-leg attack. One of the most effective and easiest involves elevating one of your opponent's legs and

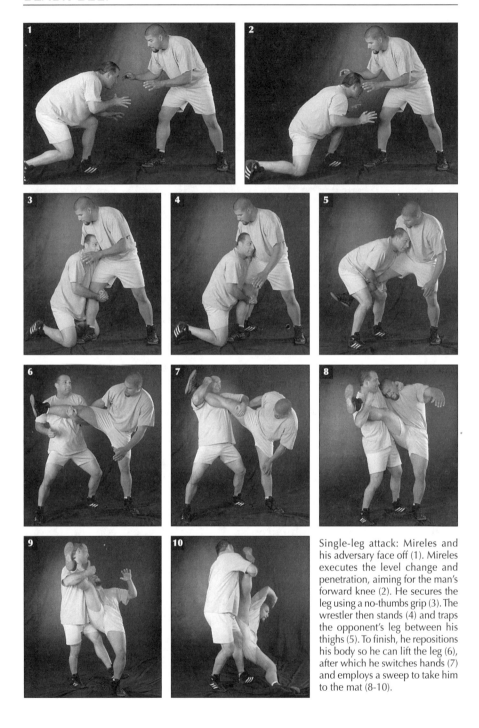

Single-leg attack: Mireles and his adversary face off (1). Mireles executes the level change and penetration, aiming for the man's forward knee (2). He secures the leg using a no-thumbs grip (3). The wrestler then stands (4) and traps the opponent's leg between his thighs (5). To finish, he repositions his body so he can lift the leg (6), after which he switches hands (7) and employs a sweep to take him to the mat (8-10).

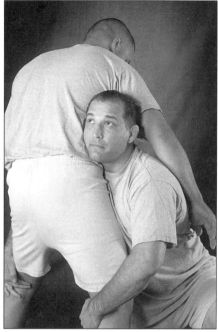

Left: Proper positioning for the single-leg attack requires the head to be up and pressing against the ribs, and the back to be straight. Right: Positioning for the double-leg attack places the shoulder and side of the head against the opponent's ribs.

sweeping the other. Because he'll be standing on one leg, you should exploit his weakened balance. Move backward (away from him) to cause him to do a split. To mitigate the discomfort, he'll begin hopping. That's your signal to move your outside hand to his heel and lift his leg as high as you can. Your action will threaten his balance and force him to draw his supporting leg close to you. From there, you can step in and sweep it with your inside leg. He'll wind up in a heap on the mat.

A Final Word

As a 21st-century martial artist, you must be well-versed in stand-up fighting, clinching and ground fighting. You'll no doubt find that double- and single-leg attacks are excellent range-transitioning techniques that can assist in bridging the gaps between those phases of fighting. Remember that mastering them is the same as it is with any other technique: Perfect practice makes perfect. With a little work and a willing partner, you'll be a leg up in no time.

SNEAKY SETUPS FOR ARMBARS
Brazilian Jujutsu Gets Devious!
by David Meyer • Photos by Rick Hustead • November 2006

If you grapple, you know that when you're battling a similarly skilled opponent, maneuvering him into a finishing hold such as the cross-body armbar can be difficult because he knows what you know—namely, that he should keep his arms in tight to avoid getting caught.

How then can you advance to the next level and teach yourself to trap a skilled opponent and finish him on the ground? There are three ways:

• **Be a better grappler.** This means you must know more than he knows, catch and hold him in positions that are difficult to escape from, force him to make mistakes and capitalize on those mistakes. To make all this happen, keep training. There's no easy or fast way to jump to this level.

• **Tire him out.** Even when someone knows the attack you're attempting, being tired or weary can make it hard for him to fend you off. You can facilitate his fatigue by fine-tuning your fitness level—so he gets tired before you do—and by being smart about how you expend your energy, resting in good positions and holding him in positions that tire him out. Again, there's no easy way to make this happen.

• **Use sneaky setups.** This strategy is one you can learn and practice right now, and it will have an immediate effect on your grappling game. That's because your opponent can't be prepared to foil your attack if he doesn't see it coming.

To start you on that third path to success, this article will present five sneaky setups for armbars: one from the guard, one from the side-control position, two from the back, and one while passing the guard. Master them, and you'll be ready to devise plenty of others on your own.

Armbar From the Guard

Source: Brazilian-*jujutsu* legend Rigan Machado of Redondo Beach, California.

Technique: It starts with a basic observation: When your opponent is in your guard and your legs are locked around his body—in what's referred to as the closed guard—he's probably aware of the danger to his limbs. Therefore, he strives to keep them bent while holding your hips down to ensure that you can't rise up and catch him in an armbar. But when you fight with your legs open or with your feet under his thighs—in the butterfly

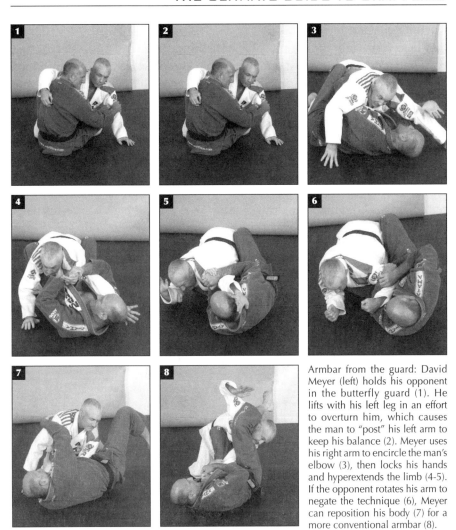

Armbar from the guard: David Meyer (left) holds his opponent in the butterfly guard (1). He lifts with his left leg in an effort to overturn him, which causes the man to "post" his left arm to keep his balance (2). Meyer uses his right arm to encircle the man's elbow (3), then locks his hands and hyperextends the limb (4-5). If the opponent rotates his arm to negate the technique (6), Meyer can reposition his body (7) for a more conventional armbar (8).

guard or two-hooks-in guard—he's much less concerned about defending his arms and much more concerned about being swept.

Therefore, start the armbar-from-the-guard technique by sitting on the mat with your adversary sitting on your feet in the butterfly guard. Extend your left arm under his right arm and around his waist. Control his left hand with your right. Lean back and onto your right side, then lift your left foot to upend him and roll him to your right.

When he senses that you're trying to control his left hand and feels his body lift, he'll fight to place that hand on the ground as a "post" to maintain his balance. At this point, you've tricked him into straightening his arm, leaving it vulnerable to attack.

Place your right hand under his left elbow, then shift your body to the right and guide his left wrist onto your right shoulder. Next, cup your hands behind his left elbow, rotating it so the bone of his elbow points up. You'll then be able to apply downward pressure to hyperextend the trapped limb in a "cutting" armbar.

This attack can fail if your opponent rotates his arm to alleviate the pain. If that happens, use your left hand to continue cupping his left arm, then pull it across to your left hip. Spin your head to the left, and with his arm deeply across your body, you'll be set up for a tight armbar. Use your right hand to hold his head down, clamp your left leg high across his back and move your right leg over the top of his head. Keep your legs heavy on him so he can't rise. Then simply drop your feet and lift your hips for the finish.

Armbar From the Side-Control Position

Source: Brazilian-jujutsu instructor John B. Will of Melbourne, Australia.

Technique: Begin in side control with your body on your opponent's

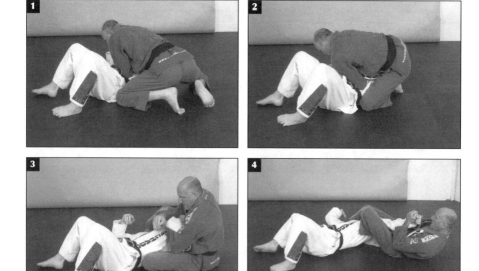

Armbar from the side-control position: Meyer starts on his opponent's left side with his left knee near his hip (1). He then disengages his left hand so he can thread it under the opponent's left wrist, after which he pivots on his left knee until his left ankle pushes against his shoulder (2). Once he swings his right leg over the man's head, he can insert his pelvis under his shoulder, squeezing with his knees (3). Meyer then lies back to straighten the limb (4).

left side. He's properly defending his arms by keeping them bent and close to his chest, between your body and his. Place your left knee on the ground near his hip. The action will free your left hand so you can slip that wrist under his left wrist. As an added distraction (or real attack), move your right forearm across his throat and threaten him with a collar choke. At this point, he's completely unaware of any armbar danger.

In one dynamic move, rotate on your left knee, bringing the inside of your left ankle against his left shoulder as you swing your right leg over his head. Sit deeply under his left shoulder with your left foot tight against your right thigh, then squeeze your knees together. His left arm is now weak and isolated, making it easy for you to grab it with one or both hands and lean back to straighten it for the tap out.

Armbar From the Back No. 1

Source: Brazilian-jujutsu master Jean Jacques Machado of Tarzana, California.

Technique: Begin in the back-control position with your legs around

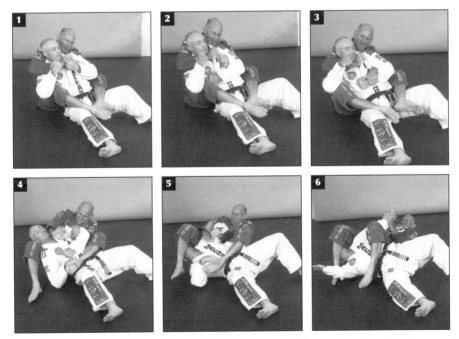

Armbar from the back No. 1: The Brazilian-jujutsu expert wraps his legs around John B. Will's torso and attempts a choke (1). He inserts his left hand under Will's left arm (2) so he can seize his wrist (3). The jujutsu stylist continues to vie for the choke using his right hand while he leans back and to his left. He repositions his right hand to push away the man's head (4). To finish, the grappler slips his right leg over Will's face (5) and executes the armbar (6).

195

your foe's hips while you and he are seated on the mat. Reach around his neck with your right hand and attempt a vigorous choke. Use your left hand, which you've extended under his left arm, to control his left wrist. As you fight for the choke with your right hand, begin leaning back and to your left. Move your feet to your opponent's right side, then fall farther to your left as you bring your left leg high across his torso. Move your right hand to the left side of his head and push him away and down as you shift your right leg over his head for the armbar.

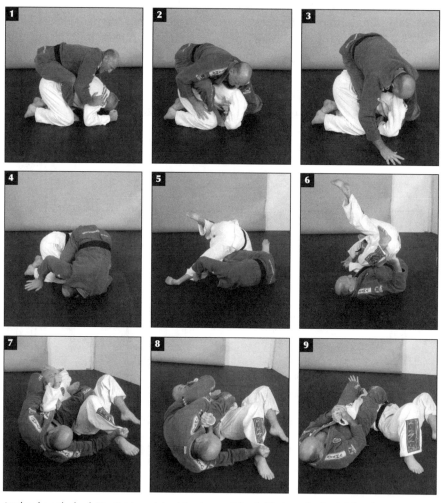

Armbar from the back No. 2: Meyer takes his adversary's back (1), then slips his left hand over the man's right shoulder and under his arm (2). Next, he repositions his left foot until his shin is against the back of his neck (3). Meyer rolls (4) and grabs the man's right pant leg (5). Moving the opponent's foot overhead, Meyer flips him (6-7). He finishes by swinging his leg over the man's face (8) to effect the armbar (9).

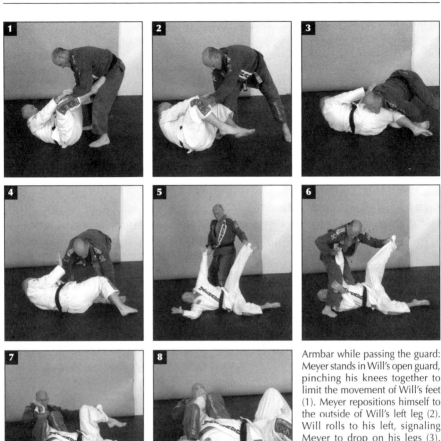

Armbar while passing the guard: Meyer stands in Will's open guard, pinching his knees together to limit the movement of Will's feet (1). Meyer repositions himself to the outside of Will's left leg (2). Will rolls to his left, signaling Meyer to drop on his legs (3). Next, he uses his right hand to grab Will's left sleeve and his left hand to grab his left pant leg (4). Meyer leaps up and lifts his opponent by the arm and leg (5). He then steps over Will's head (6) and falls into the armbar position (7). To complete the move, he lies back and extends the arm (8).

Armbar From the Back No. 2

Source: Rigan Machado.

Technique: Begin by taking your opponent's back while he's on his elbows and knees. Move your left hand across the back of his head and, coming from the top of his right shoulder, place it around and under his right arm. Reposition your left foot until your shin presses against the back of his neck and simultaneously move your right foot across his stomach. Push down with your left shin while grabbing his right pant leg with your right hand. Use your right hand to pull his foot widely over your head, lifting with your right leg to flip him. As he falls onto his back, keep hold of his pant leg to prevent him from rising to his knees in your guard. Move your left leg over his face to complete the armbar.

Armbar While Passing the Guard

Source: Rigan Machado.

Technique: Begin on your feet in your opponent's open guard. He's sitting up and using his left hand to control your right sleeve. Pinch your knees together to limit the amount his feet (his "hooks") can move you. Bend your right leg to the left to free your left leg, then reposition your left leg alongside your right as you begin to move around his guard to your right. He'll turn to his left side to improve his guard defense, and when he does, drop flat to pin his legs together. Use your right hand to grasp his left sleeve and your left hand to hold his left pant leg.

In one motion, place your hands on the ground and jump to your feet, maintaining the integrity of your grips. Thrust your hands toward the ceiling, which will result in your adversary's being lifted by his left hand and leg. That action will turn him away from you and onto his right side. Immediately step over his head with your right leg and collapse your legs to sit into an armbar on his left arm. To make the technique tight, keep your left foot against the left side of his body. If you wish, you can squeeze your thighs together, turn your knees to the right and move your left leg to the other side of his body as previously described.

These five sneaky setups for armbars will give you a real advantage over almost any opponent. Remember that in no case do you want to lose your position for a chance at a long-shot attack. That's why it's best to focus on solid, high-percentage moves like the ones described above.

BRAZILIAN JUJUTSU OVER 40
A Guide to Ground Work and Grappling
for the Working Professional

by Mark Cheng, L.Ac. • Photos by Rick Hustead • March 2007

I clearly remember my first grappling workout even though it took place more than a decade ago. After meeting the instructor for a private lesson, he told me to try to place him in a submission hold, pin or choke. We began on our feet, where I had a decent understanding of how to execute joint locks, takedowns, throws and sweeps. Once we dropped to our knees and started grappling, however, I was lost.

In the classes that followed that first lesson, I watched experienced students work to advance their skills, struggling to keep from being bested by higher belts and eager to show their own moves by forcing others to tap. I floundered as I tried to imitate the submissions the blue, purple and brown belts used. Without guidance and a progressive structure, I eventually found myself sidelined by an injury when a muscular teenager effected an ankle lock with a little too much gusto. Despite my eagerness to learn the art, perhaps Brazilian *jujutsu* wasn't for me.

Then I glanced around the academy and noticed that I wasn't the only one with an injury. Others were forcing themselves through the pain of sprained fingers, twisted ankles and other torqued joints. That got me wondering how people with active occupations or demanding lifestyles can endure such punishment over the years it takes to achieve proficiency. While every martial artist strives to persevere through incidental injuries, this seemed too risky to justify. I couldn't afford to sacrifice productivity on the job because of repeated injuries sustained while pursuing a hobby.

Back bridge with application: Brazilian-jujutsu instructor Roy Harris demonstrates the upa maneuver (1-2). He advises all his over-40 students to practice the movement because it's used in the execution of numerous jujutsu techniques, including the armbar (3).

Nor did I want to wake up 15 years later as the World's Most Dangerous Arthritic, unable to hold my grandchildren because I was too macho in my youth.

Fast-forward to the present. A San Diego-based Brazilian-jujutsu black belt named Roy Harris has invited me to his academy to show me his new training method for grappling, dubbed "Brazilian jujutsu over 40." Because I was reticent about the prospect of receiving more injuries while grappling—even though I'm in my mid-30s—I accepted with curiosity and hesitation.

I was eager to see whether Harris could present a training method for 40-plus, working professionals without sacrificing effectiveness or relying on techniques that would better suit a person who stands 6 feet 3 inches tall and weighs 200 pounds. What I saw was surprising.

Harris, known for his step-by-step delivery of often-difficult concepts, began with a white-board talk. He broke his new idea into six parts: fundamental movements, postures, positioning, techniques, escapes and training. Each part builds on the previous ones, offering students a means of developing proficiency and understanding Brazilian jujutsu in a progressive, logical manner. So far, so good, I thought.

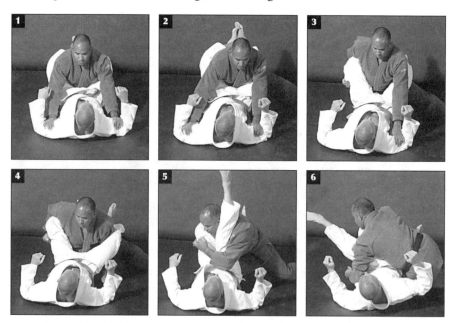

Passing the guard: Held in his opponent's guard, Harris controls the man's arms (1). He repositions his left leg for balance (2), then pins the man's left leg against his ribs to prevent him from attempting a triangle (3). Next, Harris places his left arm under the opponent's right thigh (4) and swings his leg (5) across his body to complete the escape (6).

Fundamental Movements

The first part of the course focuses on the body mechanics, strength and coordination you need to execute most of the techniques and maneuver into the positions encountered in ground grappling. For example, the back bridge (or "upa" position), the side-to-side "shrimp" position, and others that are usually taught as warm-ups or Brazilian calisthenics all have relevance as training methods because they improve coordination, balance and power.

"We've all heard people say that you can do an upa or arch your back to bump someone and destabilize him when he's mounted you," Harris says. "But you need that same body mechanic when you execute an armbar or create space from the side mount, as well. The ability to drive the hips forward is more than just a warm-up, so when you practice it, why not be aware of all the possibilities of when and how you can use that motion? In this way, the activity carries depth because of your awareness of intent and application."

Postures

Harris continues with instruction in defensive postures. "Young guys in their 20s do plenty of attacking, so let them attack," he says. "We'll work on our defenses, and eventually, after they waste their energy trying for the hot-shot techniques, they'll make mistakes and give us openings. But to get to that point, you need to have solid defenses."

To address that need, he focuses on three basic defensive positions designed for the three main positions of vulnerability in Brazilian jujutsu: the mount, side mount and guard.

Defensive posturing revolves around using positions to buy time to create escapes or otherwise capitalize on your opponent's mistakes. "As a 40-something-year-old, you have to face the reality that your body may not have the same endurance, strength or resilience as the buff 20-year-old you're grappling with," Harris says.

To highlight his points, Harris demonstrates the postures with one of his younger brown belts, who is told to attack at full speed on the ground. In each case, he assumes a defensive posture while the student works to effect a submission. However, when one position fails to yield a fruitful outcome, the brown belt moves to a different one. At that moment, Harris capitalizes on the transition by pushing his opponent off and standing up, by sweeping him or by executing a submission.

Positioning

Slightly different from posturing, positioning incorporates the defensive postures and fundamental movements in ways that further destabilize the opponent or nullify his attacks. It develops your understanding of how to position your legs, hips, arms and head to achieve those ends.

To illustrate, Harris has his partner pull him into his guard, after which he simply sits back on his right shin and instep, and spreads his knees for stability. The sole of his left foot is close to his buttocks, and his left knee is high to obstruct his opponent's hip. His spine stays straight, and his elbows are pulled inward and kept close to his ribs.

"My goal is to keep his left foot off my hip," Harris says. "I don't worry about his other foot because I haven't left him any room to get to a position of control or leverage on my left hip. Now I can sit back, use my hands and elbows to keep his feet from gaining leverage over my body, and wait for him to give me an opportunity to pass his guard by simply putting my left knee down over his left thigh for an early Christmas present."

He punctuates his statement by snatching the brown belt's left ankle for a foot lock.

Techniques

Brazilian jujutsu has combinations of moves designed to meet the needs of grapplers—needs that include moving from a position of inferiority to a position of neutrality or advantage. "It's very simple," Harris says. "If you end up on the bottom of someone's mount, you want to escape by placing him in your guard. If you end up in his guard, you want to side-mount him. If he has you on the bottom of a side mount, you want to go to your knees or replace the guard.

"As far as submissions go, you're just looking for the highest-percentage techniques that work for people with smaller or lighter builds—not the crazy, flying arm locks that look like they came off a highlights reel. If this were Brazilian jujutsu for teens or pro fighters, that's one thing; but people who have only a couple of hours a week to train generally don't have time to develop those highly athletic techniques."

The bent-arm locks (*kimura* and "paintbrush"), the guillotine choke and the heel hook are the mainstays of Harris' course. "You may be wondering where the straight-arm lock and rear-naked choke are," he says. "Let me remind you that we must first focus on the highest-percentage techniques that are still readily executed by people with minimal strength and athleticism."

Escapes

Harris identifies two easy-to-exploit situations in which you can apply an escape in Brazilian jujutsu. The first occurs when your opponent drives his weight down and into you with his legs, hips and lower back. The second occurs when he shifts his weight off your body and onto his legs or knees to change position.

Preventing the armbar: The opponent mounts Harris (1). When Harris pushes up on the man's chest (2), he traps Harris' left arm and repositions his body for an armbar (3). Harris immediately grabs the opponent's right knee (4) and maneuvers his head out from under it (5). With his head free, Harris turns to face his foe in the guard (6).

Escapes are to Brazilian jujutsu as apologies are to conversation. If you find yourself in a position in which you've upset someone, the easiest way out is simply to assuage his wrath. In grappling, if you find yourself

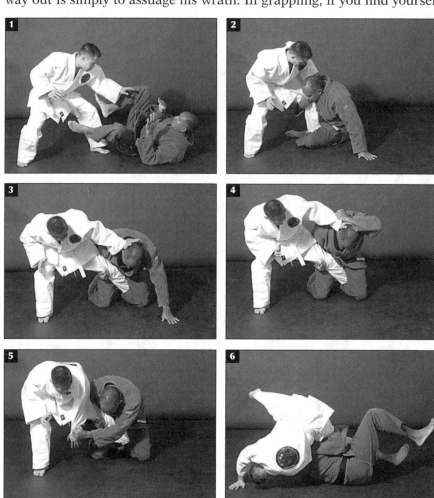

Rolling takedown: Harris lies on his back as Mark Cheng approaches (1). As soon as he's within reach, Harris seizes his closest leg with his right arm and left leg (2). He rocks onto his knees to straighten the man's leg (3), then uses his left hand to remove Cheng's left arm from his head (4-5). Next, Harris rolls forward to flip him (6). With Cheng on his back, Harris climbs to the side-control position (7).

in a vulnerable position in which you're about to be submitted, the most efficient way out is to effect an escape so your opponent no longer has you in a position of inferiority or your limb is no longer in a position of jeopardy.

"The basic escapes you'll need most are from the straight armbar, the bent-arm locks and the triangle," says Harris, who also holds a senior full instructor rank in *jeet kune do*. Some of the nullifications he teaches are so simple that they can be taught in seconds. For example, if you find yourself in your opponent's guard and he attempts a bent-arm lock, you can often neutralize it by turning your fingers outward and corkscrewing your elbow inward toward your ribs. That keeps your weight back on your base and prevents him from gaining leverage over your limb.

Training

Also known as "rolling," training is the free-form phase of grappling in which you can use all the concepts, skills, abilities and techniques you've learned in the earlier stages of training. However, the most important thing to remember is also the easiest to forget.

It's tempting to get caught up in the adrenaline rush of rolling and go full speed ahead, but the older and wiser grappler will remember that the defensive postures, positions and escapes are what set him apart from his younger, more aggressive opponent. While the defensive game is certainly not the most eye-catching, it does make you less prone to injury by minimizing the openings that you'd otherwise present to your opponent and by allowing you to conserve energy instead of fighting speed-on-speed and strength-on-strength.

No matter your age or ability, following Harris' training method will get you back to the mat without fear of injury. More important, it will provide you with a way of preserving your life outside the *dojo*—without having injuries to heal and frustrations to overcome.

GRAPPLING GUIDE
When to Go to the Ground and When to Stay on Your Feet

by John B. Will • Photos by Rick Hustead • April 2007

In the late 1980s, I accompanied Rigan Machado to Rio de Janeiro, Brazil, for a month's training on the mat. At the time, very few in the States and almost no one here in Australia had heard of this now-popular system. Back then, you'd be lucky to find a grappling article in any martial arts magazine. Now, we're seeing whole issues devoted to the topic. Times certainly have changed.

As a result of the increased awareness of the effectiveness of grappling and the demand for instruction in ground fighting, instructors are crawling out of the woodwork. A few have something good to offer, many have a very limited knowledge of the subject but, unfortunately, most don't have a clue. The silver lining is that more and more martial artists seem willing to broaden their horizons and are doing all they can to find out more about grappling.

In this article, I'll offer advice for both camps—that is, more information for those who have a genuine interest in grappling and something for those who feel threatened by it and believe that it somehow devalues their investment in the art they already practice.

When Grappling Is Appropriate

• **The Challenge:** In a one-on-one contest between two people, whether it stems from a serious disagreement or is aimed at determining the effectiveness of the style or the fighter, grappling can be a winning strategy. The reasons are many, but the main one is that once the parties hit the ground, which will often happen, the person with all his years invested in stand-up fighting will be left with nothing to do. The grappler, however, will be ready to go to work. It's that simple.

What many martial artists find objectionable is the very idea that they can be taken down in the first place. "But I would just kick him in the groin, and that would be that," they say. Ever tried that, with maybe $20 riding on the outcome? Even with a partner who believes the same thing, it's an eye-opener. Word of advice: Be ready to part with those hard-earned dollars because taking someone down is easier than you think.

The reason people are frequently shocked by the fact that they can't knock out their opponent before he clinches is they simply have never

Author John B. Will demonstrates three easy-to-assume postures that grapplers can use to protect themselves against a strike.

trained to avoid the clinch. Most people just play the same game their partner plays—i.e., *taekwondo* stylists agree to stand apart and throw techniques at each other, and *karateka*, boxers and kickboxers do likewise. Most students of the fighting arts don't train to stop an assailant who genuinely wants to rush in and grab hold of them. Hence the big surprise when it happens.

The reality: In many no-rules encounters, the grappler will clinch before the knockout occurs. If that happens, the pure stand-up fighter has everything stacked against him.

Best bets: For the stand-up fighter, move and throw shots with KO potential. Don't hesitate. For the grappler, cover up, work your distance well, commit to the clinch and crash in hard.

• **The Arrest:** Provided it's not a one-against-many altercation, grappling is an appropriate answer for many situations that arise when laws are being enforced. Officers cannot afford to stand back and punch it out with an offender for several reasons:

It can take too long, thereby allowing other suspects to get away or, even worse, prepare themselves for deadly resistance.

It's more court- and media-friendly to grapple with an offender and make an arrest than it is to beat him into submission—even though he may be resisting violently.

Grappling is more efficient, making the altercation less likely to develop into a three-round bloodfest. It's more likely to end within a short time.

Once brought to the ground, the struggle is contained in a single location. In contrast, a stand-up fight may take the officer away from his support network—i.e., car, radio, other officers and so on.

The Rodney King incident is a perfect example. If the officers had been allowed to apply a choke or some other grappling move, the situation

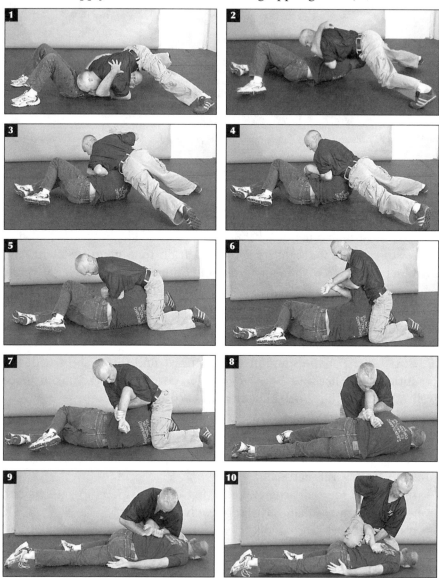

The arrest: Jujutsu stylist Will controls the suspect from the top (1). Having seized the man's left arm, Will begins moving his legs to his left side and rolls him onto his right shoulder (2-3). The grappler uses his right hand to control the opponent's left wrist (4) as he repositions his knees to trap his head (5). Will twists his torso to leverage the limb behind the man's back (6-7), then scoots to his opposite side (8). From there, he turns the suspect onto his stomach and pins his arm behind his back (9) so he can begin the handcuffing procedure (10).

The attempted rape: The author normally doesn't advise women to grapple with male attackers, but if they're already on the ground with a man on top of them, collar chokes such as this one can be effective.

would have ended in seconds. Millions of dollars would have been saved in court costs.

Several months before I started writing this article, I witnessed an offender breeze through three security guards in a few seconds. He was well over 6 feet tall and obviously more "motivated" than the guards who were trying to arrest him. He took off down the street, with the one guard in pursuit. I intervened by driving ahead of him and taking him down as he barreled toward me on the sidewalk. The arrest took all of 10 seconds, and he was strapped up and handed over to the security guards. A slugfest with that man would have been extremely inefficient and could have resulted in a lawsuit because I was making a citizen's arrest based solely on what I'd seen take place. It was a perfect example of when grappling and control techniques are a better answer than a knockout.

The reality: Making an arrest is a hands-on procedure. A noncompliant offender can rarely be made compliant by hitting him. A compliant offender can also have a change of heart and turn noncompliant once the gap has been closed, leaving grappling as the only option.

Best bets: Take the suspect down and apply controls and/or a choke to effect the arrest.

• **The Attempted Rape:** Although women should avoid grappling at all costs—unless they're highly skilled—I've included this scenario here because in most attempted rapes, the woman has no choice. If a rape is in progress, the woman is already on the ground and the clinch has taken place.

Most rapes occur in the home and are perpetrated by a man the victim knows. Rarely will standing back and slamming home a kick or punch save the day. It's usually in close quarters, and disengaging can be more difficult than you think. In this situation, good ground skills and some simple chokes that will render an attacker unconscious within a few seconds will serve you more effectively than strikes. It's easy to put an adversary to sleep from the bottom position, particularly when he has little or no knowledge of ground work. Choking is the most efficient way to stop a larger, stronger and more motivated assailant.

The reality: Rapes and assaults on women usually occur at "nose length," where kicking and punching seldom work. Once you're on the floor, grappling is the answer—to effect a positional change that will allow you to escape or to effect a choke or break that will terminate the threat.

Best bets: Fight, fight, fight! Choke him out, then run.

• **The No-Choice Scenario:** This one is simple—it's appropriate to grapple when you're on the ground and have no other choice. If you practice with self-defense and effectiveness in mind, this is the most compelling argument for acquiring skill at grappling. If you have no real interest in grappling or wrestling, at least learn the basics for the worst-case scenario.

I've heard testimony from many martial artists who've described their battles using phrases like, "We were too close to do anything," "We ended up on the ground," and "It wasn't like sparring in the dojo." The

The crowded-place scenario: Because a bystander may feel compelled to help the person that appears to be losing in a ground fight, Will (pointing) says grappling should be avoided when other people are present.

210

last sentence holds the key, for sparring is very different from fighting. In sparring, two people usually agree to stay at a convenient range and not go all out. Another distinguishing characteristic is that in sparring, it's usually difficult to determine the winner. Grappling, on the other hand, more often than not has a clear winner. It's usually performed all out, and after a bit of practice, the nitty-gritty of "too close" and "too nasty" seems comfortable and normal.

The sensible approach for the stand-up fighter is not to say, "I don't want to grapple; I'll win all my fights by KO." It's to say, "I will learn a little about it just in case."

The reality: It's rarely your choice to grapple. It's up to the environment, the situation and the other guy. Therefore, you should learn how to function on the ground.

Best bets: Considering that most people don't know anything about ground work, learning only a little will give you a big advantage. You may even have fun. If you won't pursue it, remember that if you do hit the ground, your best strategy is to stay as close to your opponent as possible. That way, fewer bad things will happen to you. If you manage to get on top, use head butts and elbow strikes.

When Grappling Isn't Appropriate

• **The Multiple-Attacker Scenario:** When you're alone and facing more than one opponent, it's not advisable to go to ground. You may well end up there anyway, so you should be able to try something. I've taught several people who work in the security industry, and on occasion, they've borne the brunt of an attack by half a dozen assailants. They reported that in some cases, the sheer number of assailants drove them down and they could do nothing to stay on their feet.

Some went on to say that on several such occasions, they emerged fairly unscathed. The problem for the bad guys was that too many were trying to do the same thing, which positioned them in each others' way. Also, in several incidents, the grapplers said they were able to choke out one or more of the aggressors while fighting from the bottom—which meant they were somewhat protected from a third-party attack.

The reality: Don't choose to go to the ground when facing more than one attacker. Do what you can to win on your feet. Still, three or four determined aggressors will almost always be able to get you on the floor.

Best bets: If you do go down under the weight of numbers, get under one of them. Then keep him close and use his body as a shield. Try to

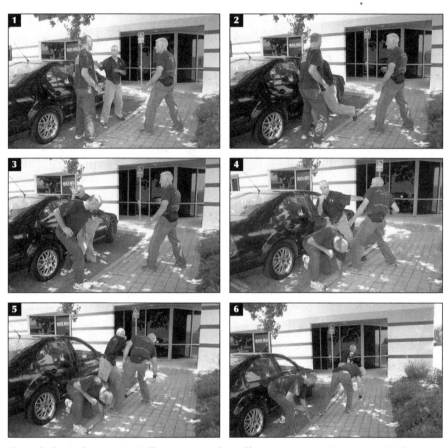

The multiple-attacker scenario: Will (center) is confronted by two aggressors (1). He immediately slams a low kick into the first man's lead leg (2-3), then smashes his fist into the second man's face (4-5) and flees (6). If he'd chosen to grapple with one of them, the other surely would have joined the altercation.

choke him out from that position. Once he's neutralized, move on to the next one.

• **The Crowded-Place Scenario:** If you're fighting one adversary in a place where there are many people who don't know you, it's inadvisable to go to the ground. The reason is human nature: Every now and then, some innocent bystander will intervene and cause you grief in his efforts to save the other guy.

This has happened to me. Once, when I'd mounted my attacker and was busy putting him away, an onlooker came to his rescue. I then had to deal with him in a like manner, for once he was under way, there was no stopping him with words.

The reality: Sometimes people don't care who starts an altercation; they just want to stop the guy who's winning.

Best bets: Should you find yourself in such a situation, finish your opponent quickly and disengage. Or move under him and finish him from there while you mislead onlookers into thinking he's winning because he's on top.

Final Considerations

Don't take a fight to the ground unless:

• You know something about grappling/wrestling, or

• You're taking a beating on your feet and have no choice but to try to equalize the odds.

BRAZILIAN JUJUTSU MADE BETTER
3 Wrestling Techniques That Will Supercharge Your Self-Defense

by Mark Mireles • Photos by Rick Hustead • May 2007

Whether you call it "cross-training," a "hybrid approach" or "mixed martial arts," your goal is clear: to diversify your skills by adopting techniques from other styles of fighting. And to anyone with experience in the martial arts, your reasoning is equally clear: Because nothing is perfect, all systems of combat can be improved.

Throughout the history of the martial arts, many masters have recognized this. Bruce Lee was one of them. Sensing the shortcomings of his original art, he studied other styles from the East and a few from the West. He learned new theories and techniques and tested them before creating what's now regarded as one of the premier fighting systems on the planet: *jeet kune do.*

Another pioneer was Imi Lichtenfeld, founder of the Israeli art of *Krav Maga.* He developed his system for survival on the battlefield. Like Lee, Lichtenfeld researched various fighting arts and extracted what he believed would be the most relevant for his soldiers. Over time, Krav Maga developed further, making it functional for police officers and civilians.

The newest pioneers in the martial arts are Brazilian-*jujutsu* practitioners. Using the methods the Gracie family learned from a Japanese judo champion, they created what's arguably the most effective grappling system in the world.

Can these three successful hybrid arts be improved? Of course. While you're reading this, experts in each art are probably analyzing and fine-tuning their methods. Since my expertise is in wrestling, I'll leave the analysis of JKD and Krav Maga to others and concentrate on what I know—specifically, on how American wrestling can be used to augment Brazilian jujutsu.

Cousin Arts

Although Brazilian jujutsu and wrestling are both systems of hand-to-hand combat that are effective on the ground, they use very different approaches. Jujutsu uses fluidity and suppleness, whereas wrestling often relies on direct aggression. Wrestling has a multitude of attacks executed from the standing position, while jujutsu is less well-versed there. Jujutsu exponents strive to master the science of submission and strangulation,

The switch: Mark Mireles begins on his hands and knees with his opponent on his back (1). He places his left arm across his right so he can use it as a post (2), then turns while repositioning his left leg (3). The wrestler raises his right arm before leveraging it downward to apply pressure to the man's right shoulder (4). Next, he controls his right arm as he turns clockwise (5) and makes his way to the man's back (6-7).

while wrestlers focus on subjugation techniques and, if they're into MMA, the ground-and-pound method.

There's an ideological divide between the two systems, but are they really at the opposite ends of the spectrum? No. A review of the techniques of both arts reveals how easily they can supplement each other in combat. This article will teach three wrestling techniques that can boost the effectiveness of Brazilian jujutsu. They pertain to common positions in which the jujutsu exponent can find himself. Although the Brazilian art teaches methods of escape and reversal for each position, I'll present new options drawn from wrestling.

The Switch

The switch is a reversal that starts from one of the least desirable positions in grappling: when your attacker has taken your back. Start on your hands and knees in a base position, and expect that your opponent will have his hands wrapped around your waist in some sort of lock.

Your goal is to effect two actions simultaneously: Clear your near hand over your far hand, placing your arms in a position that resembles an "X." Then raise your far knee and pass your near leg under your far leg. Your near hand is now planted on the ground, creating a "post." Your far arm leaves the ground and moves close to your body. Raise your butt off the ground, balancing on your feet and your post (near hand). This motion will allow you to turn your hips 180 degrees and begin the reversal. Note that at the beginning of the switch, your pelvis is facing the ground. If you execute the two aforementioned steps correctly, your pelvis will face upward.

The second phase of the switch involves using your far arm to apply pressure to the attacker's far shoulder. This action also creates a fulcrum, allowing you to take his back. To do it, bend the arm you cleared and use it to smash his far shoulder. Quickly extend your arm, reaching your hand deep between his legs to increase your leverage on his shoulder. Your goal isn't to break the lock but to lock his shoulder into a secure position.

When you reach into his crotch area, secure your hand on the thigh closest to you with your palm facing up. To create a fulcrum at your attacker's shoulder, continue to place your weight on it. Simultaneously attempt to curl your arm as it's planted on his inner thigh. Your butt is still raised, which allows you to place your weight on his shoulder.

The final phase is accomplished by swinging your far leg over your opponent's back in a high arcing motion. The fulcrum you create will facilitate your taking his back. Once you're on top, the reversal is compete.

The Inside-Leg Stand-Up

Brazilian jujutsu embraces the strategy of keeping your opponent on the ground and finishing him there with chokes and submissions. However, many hand-to-hand combat instructors advocate getting off the ground as soon as possible, arguing that it's especially important if you're the one on the bottom. They teach that the optimal position of control occurs when your attacker is on the ground and you're on your feet.

The inside-leg stand-up: James Walsh takes Mireles' back (1). Mireles "builds up" by raising his left leg while grabbing the man's wrists (2). Having covered his opponent's hands, Mireles rises to his feet and pushes backward against the man's chest (3). To escape, he moves his left leg forward while pulling apart his opponent's hands (4). The wrestler then places the man's left hand against his own left hip and pivots (5). The motion puts him in position for a counterattack (6-7).

One technique that can help you get off the deck and into a better position is the inside-leg stand-up. Consider it a worst-case-scenario technique for use when the fight has gone to the ground and your attacker has your back.

You're in a base position, and your opponent has a lock around your waist. You must immediately explode upward. This process, called "building up," may require tenacious second and third efforts. To build up, you need to execute two independent but related actions. For the first, power up by raising your near leg and planting your foot on the ground a little more

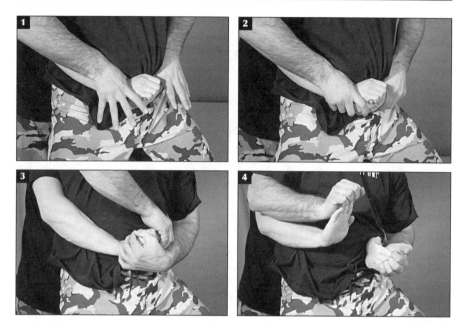

Up close and personal: Mireles drills his thumbs into the gap between his stomach and his opponent's wrists while pushing his hips forward (1). As the opponent's arms are straightened, his grip weakens (2). Mireles then uses his left hand to cover the man's top hand and his right to pry off his fingers (3). To prevent a counterattack, he holds onto his fingers after the hold has been broken (4).

than 45 degrees to the side. Look up, then raise your torso so your back and head are vertical. You should be pushing slightly into your attacker, not pulling away from him. As you began to rise, you should have covered his hand with your hands.

As your inside leg carries you upward, rise to your feet by "rolling" your far foot. Accomplish that by using an outward rolling motion from your current position of full outside-leg flexion. As you roll your foot and knee, extend your leg and plant your far foot on the ground. Then rise while continuing to push backward into your attacker. The only thing holding you at this point is his hands locked around you. You need to exploit his grip—which you do by pushing back into him while keeping your knees slightly bent and pressing your hips forward. This action puts pressure on his lock and extends his arms.

You're now up but not out because your adversary's lock on your waist is preventing you from escaping. To get back into the fight, you have to break free and face him. When you came up on your inside leg, you covered his hands with your own; you must now break his grip. First, move either leg slightly forward while maintaining your balance. Second, move his grip toward the hip that just moved forward. Next, dig your thumbs between your stomach and his inner wrists while thrusting your hips forward. As his arms straighten, his grip will weaken.

Cover his top hand and use your same-side hand to pry up his four fingers. Recruit your free hand to lift his other hand. To minimize the chance of being counterattacked, keep hold of his digits as you pull his lock apart and move your hips forward. Place his far hand against your far hip—it's called "putting his hand in your back pocket"—and turn toward it to face him.

The Short Sit-Out and Roll

This basic technique exists in the arsenal of the jujutsu practitioner,

The short sit-out and roll: Mireles establishes a base, and his opponent locks his arms around his torso (1). Mireles uses his right hand to grasp his adversary's hands (2) and executes a short sit-out (3). Pushing with his legs, he maintains backward pressure (4). When the opponent tries to resist by pushing forward, Mireles repositions his legs (5) and begins his roll while gripping the opponent's right hand (6). The man winds up on his back (7), and Mireles lands on top of him (8). From there, he can turn to achieve side control (9).

but wrestling teaches a variation called the short sit-out. It starts with your opponent at your back with a lock around your waist. You must initiate two actions simultaneously: Cover his lock with your far hand and execute the short sit-out. That entails starting in the base position and sitting on your butt while keeping your head and spine upright. Keep your back toward your opponent's chest. Dig your heels into the ground and push backward to maximize his discomfort. To compensate, he'll attempt to reposition himself by moving forward—which is your cue to roll.

As he pushes forward, quickly return to a base position at a 90-degree angle in front of him. Maintain your far-side grip on his locked hand. Some wrestlers execute this move by grabbing their opponent's wrist or forearm so they can create a hook with their elbow when they roll; however, that can telegraph your intentions. The preferred method is to cover the four fingers of his hand and squeeze hard, then use your hips to create a fulcrum under his torso.

Your next task is to load him onto your hips. He's pinned there because of your grip on his hand and the outside position of his arm. Holding his hand tight, roll onto your outside hip and shoulder. He'll be forced to roll, as well, and land on his back, leaving you in a more advantageous position from which you can easily dominate him.

3 FACETS OF GRAPPLING
John Machado Explains Why You Need to Know Them All

by Robert W. Young • Photos by Rick Hustead • June 2007

As more and more martial artists recognize the value of augmenting their self-defense skills with grappling, we at *Black Belt* thought an overview of the various categories of techniques was in order. So with help from Brazilian-*jujutsu* master John Machado, one of the top grappling authorities in the United States, we offer the following examination of the big three: pain-compliance techniques, breaking techniques and choking techniques.

Man, That Hurts!

"Pain is one of the tools available to you in grappling, but it has limitations because a lot of people don't feel pain," Machado says. "Sometimes when you try a pain-compliance technique on someone's arm, leg or neck, he'll feel nothing. He doesn't have to be drunk or on drugs; he just doesn't feel it."

Fortunately, pain-compliance techniques work most of the time—approximately 70 percent, Machado estimates.

The majority of the moves function by crushing a muscle or extending a joint in an uncomfortable direction, Machado says. "The biceps lock works by 'cutting' the muscle. Another technique might work by extending the elbow, knee or neck to cause pain. The side neck crank is a good example. You don't want to break the neck; you want to cause pain by hurting the neck muscles."

In schools that teach leg locks, the calf crush is a popular pain-compliance technique. "You can do a foot lock on the ankle, or you can hold the calf and 'cut' it," Machado says. "A lot of people will tap right there. Just remember that for some, there's no effect."

He advises martial artists to avoid spending an undue amount of time trying to make a pain-compliance technique work. "When you apply a hold, watch your opponent's reaction," he says. "If you see him lifting his hand to tap, it's a sign the lock is working. Otherwise, quickly move to a different hold."

During that short period in which you're gauging the effectiveness of the move, limit the amount of effort you exert. "You shouldn't go 100 percent because you never know for sure that the lock is even going to work or

221

Break: John Machado controls his opponent from the top (1). He grabs the man's right wrist (2) and pushes it to the mat (3), then slips his right arm under the opponent's upper arm (4). Once his right hand is locked onto his left wrist, Machado lifts the shoulder and pushes the trapped hand toward the man's head (5). The breaking technique targets the shoulder.

whether he'll counter it," Machado says. "You should apply the technique and use enough pressure to make it work. You know from practicing it in the *dojo* how much force that requires—how much effort it takes in a perfect situation. If it doesn't have an effect, just move on."

Pain-compliance techniques will serve you well in training and self-defense, Machado says. Before you try them in a tournament, though, find out if they're permitted.

There Goes the Arm!

Breaking techniques target the body's joints, not the bones. Some of them are so cleverly designed that they attack more than one body part at the same time.

"When you do a triangle choke, for example, you're doing a neck crank, a choke and an armbar," Machado says. "You can finish your opponent with all of them together.

"The *kimura* usually targets the shoulder, but it can also attack the arm with an inverted armbar. It depends on the angle."

The most efficient breaking techniques use both of your arms against one of your opponent's limbs. The strength differential makes it relatively easy for you to hyperextend the joint, rupturing the ligaments and even breaking the bone. "The techniques are even more effective when you have your whole body working against one joint—whether it's a knee, wrist or elbow," Machado says.

In breaking, leverage is everything. "Without it, you can't do the moves because jujutsu is based on leverage," Machado adds.

Many attempts at executing one of the most popular breaking techniques—the cross-body armbar—fail because the fulcrum, or the part of your body against which the opponent's arm is forced, isn't slightly above the elbow. "If you do it that way, you don't have the lock," Machado says. "You're putting pressure on the bone. You need to switch to a different technique quickly because if you don't, he'll escape."

Breaking techniques are good for self-defense, but before attempting one, you must determine whether the situation will permit you to safely execute it. "You don't want to use an armbar in a fight in a nightclub with hundreds of people around," Machado says. "Every technique has its place, and that's not the right one for an armbar."

Likewise, if you're in law enforcement, you probably don't want to take a suspect down and break his arm because of the legal issues involved, Machado says. "You'd probably be better off using a short armbar to make him cooperate with the handcuffing procedure or subduing him with pain compliance."

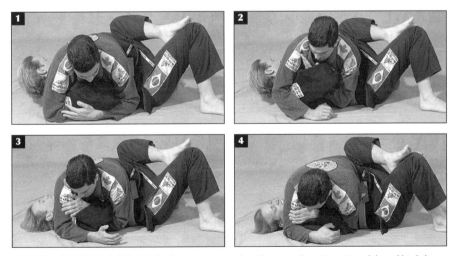

Pain: If the shoulder lock fails, Machado can return to the side-control position (1) and thread his left arm inside the opponent's bent limb (2-3). He then wraps his fingers around his own right biceps and applies a pain-compliance technique that puts pressure on the elbow (4).

Pain: If the lock shown on the previous page doesn't have the desired effect, Machado can re-establish side control (1). From there, he extends his right leg and shifts his body toward his opponent's legs (2). Machado then moves his left arm so it lies across the man's chest, clasps his hands and applies a neck crank (3).

In epic battles, just how debilitating is a broken limb? "In any form of combat, you have to deal with adrenaline and the fight-or-flight reaction," Machado says. "Sometimes a person doesn't realize that his arm is broken until the end of the match, so he keeps on fighting back. That's why, in some respects, chokes are superior."

Wake Me When It's Over!

The fighting arts teach two types of choking techniques: air and blood. "You can suffocate someone to death if you squeeze the throat, or you can subdue him the right way, which is by squeezing the arteries on the sides of his neck so blood stops flowing to his brain," Machado says.

It's obviously imperative to learn the difference. "You should never do a choke against the windpipe because you can kill your opponent," he says. The key to making your technique attack the arteries is to make a V-shape with your arm and position his windpipe in the crook of your elbow, he adds.

Once you begin applying pressure, it takes about three to five seconds for unconsciousness to follow.

Blood chokes can be effected with your arm or your opponent's uniform. "Both are very important in grappling and very effective," Machado says. "The arm choke is powerful. You can do it while wearing a *gi* or while not wearing one, so it works in a variety of situations. You can be on the beach in Rio and get into a fight and choke someone out using your arms. Or you can be in a cage tournament and use the same move."

But the key to success in self-defense, he says, is learning how to execute the choke with the collar. "It's more useful because everybody is wearing something—a shirt, a jacket, a uniform," he says. "Even a T-shirt can work. There's a chance it'll rip, but if you know how to grip it deep and pull, you'll have a better chance of making it work. The thing to remember is, if you can get your hand in deep enough to grab the T-shirt right, you can probably do an arm choke. It's all about being versatile."

When it comes to choking, builders of bulging biceps beware: Skinny arms are easier to insert into tight spaces such as the gap between a resisting opponent's head and shoulder or chin and chest, and bony limbs make the constriction more immediate. "And if your biceps are too big, it's hard to even get your arms in deep enough," he says.

Self-defense caveat: Depending on the state or country in which you live, you may want to forgo all-out choking as a self-defense strategy because juries often misinterpret it as an attempt to kill. "It's better to use a choke to restrain someone than it is to render him unconscious," Machado says. "A choke is like a gun: You cannot use it on everybody who assaults you."

Believe it or not, there are people who are immune to some choking techniques, Machado says. "It's very rare, but I've encountered martial artists who cannot be choked out. One was a friend of mine in Brazil: Renaldo, an old-time black belt under the Gracies. When we would see

Choke: In side control, Machado wraps his right arm around the opponent's neck and grabs his collar (1). Machado then places his left knee on the man's abdomen (2) and secures the right side of his collar with his free hand (3). To finish, the jujutsu master leans away from the man's head and uses his arms to exert pressure against the arteries on the sides of his neck (4).

him, he would say, 'Come and test your choke.' He would give us his neck, and we couldn't choke him because of the way his body was built.

"At my school in Culver City, California, I have one student like that. If you try a collar choke or cross choke on him, your grip will get tired before you beat him. With a full back choke, though, he'll tap."

If you ever encounter an opponent who's resistant to chokes, Machado says, follow the same principle described above and move on to an armbar or some other grappling technique.

Pain and break: From the side-control position, Machado moves his left leg over the opponent's torso (1). He controls the man's left arm (2) before swinging his right leg over his head (3-4). Machado then sits back and executes a pain-compliance technique on the trapped arm (5). If the hold fails to effect a submission, Machado can lie back (6) and lock on an armbar (7).

B.J. PENN
The Ultimate Fighter's Newest Coach Reveals His Training and Fighting Secrets!
by Edward Pollard • Photos by Rick Hustead • June 2007

In the world of mixed martial arts, it's not hard to spot a winner. He's usually holding a big, shiny belt and covered with sweat—and often the blood of his opponent. Some winners are different, and they find satisfaction in other ways. Take B.J. Penn, for instance. After making his mark in 2001 as a lightweight in the Ultimate Fighting Championship 31, he's fought in practically every weight class, including heavyweight, and has beaten tough opponents every step of the way. His biggest recent win in the UFC came against Matt Hughes in 2004, who until then had ruled the welterweight division. Penn tested the waters of K-1 in Japan and Rumble on the Rock in his home state of Hawaii before returning to the UFC. In 2006 he fought a rematch with Hughes at the UFC 63. Penn dominated the first two rounds, then lost his momentum and the fight after an awkward injury. It was that loss, however, that cleared his schedule and allowed him to coach opposite his old nemesis, Jens Pulver, in Season 5 of The Ultimate Fighter. Black Belt spoke to Penn at the UFC training center in Las Vegas only days before the shooting of the hit reality-TV series wrapped.

—E.P.

Black Belt: You were introduced to *jujutsu* by Tom Callos. Did you feel that it offered you secrets for gaining more control in a fight?

B.J. Penn: I never thought about it as secrets; I thought of it as knowledge. I needed to know as much as I could at all times, and I always try to learn. I consider myself the forever student. I believe I'm the best, but I can never stop learning. You have to go to all the good people out there and learn what they know, whether it's swapping techniques or just being a straight-up student. Once you forget that, you're done. All you can do is train every single day and hope you're current with what's going on because things move so fast.

BB: It must be difficult to stay current once you've risen to the top of the mixed martial arts. What methods do you use?

Penn: I train in jujutsu all the time. I do some weights and some cardiovascular, and I stretch a lot and do plyometrics. Nutrition is important; you've got to eat the right foods. You've got to have a nutritionist or a friend who knows nutrition because if you're just working out and not eating right, you're wasting your time. Once you stop watching your nutrition, it ruins everything. Your body starts breaking down immediately. You have to combine hard training with proper nutrition. You learn so much faster because your brain functions better when it has better food.

BB: What's your training regimen when you're preparing for a fight?

Penn: I've done it all. I've gone six hours a day with three two-hour sessions. I've tried one hour a day. For this next fight [with Jens Pulver], I'm probably going to go three hours in the morning and an hour and a half at night.

BB: Do you tailor your training to your opponent?

Penn: No, it's just my normal 100 percent raised to a higher level. My 100 used to be one hour a day every other day, but now my 100 is train in the morning, sleep all day and train at night. I really like that long break in the middle.

BB: How do you develop your endurance?

Penn: There are different ways—the most basic is keeping your heart rate at 70 percent to 75 percent for a certain amount of time using a heart-rate monitor. I run on a treadmill, bike uphill or do whatever gets my heart pumping. Sprints are important for engaging the anaerobic system. I run

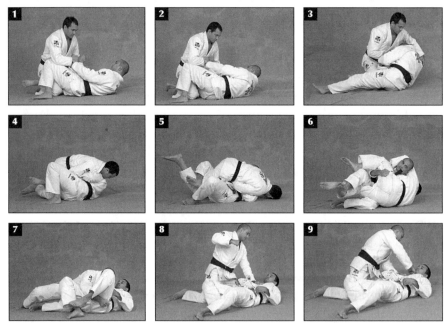

From his back: With his opponent in his half-guard, B.J. Penn controls the man's right arm (1). Penn turns onto his right side (2) and sits up (3). The opponent leans forward to oppose Penn's motion, which causes the jujutsu expert to reverse directions and use his energy against him (4). Penn rolls the man onto his back (5-6) and establishes side control (7), after which he finishes with a punch (8-9).

laps underwater and do 500-yard sprints. I hate sprints, but I know I have to do them.

You can also do circuit training: sprint 40 yards forward, 40 yards backward, jump 10 times, walk [in a] wheelbarrow 10 yards forward and 10 yards backward, jump off your hands left and right, then do skipping back and forth. Try to build your aerobic base and start working the sprints in. It's better to just stay in shape all year round and always be your best. When you drop out of it and then try to get ready for a fight in two months, you have to start all over. If your opponent's near your skill level and he stayed in shape all the time, he'll have the advantage.

BB: You're known for your flexibility. What role does stretching play in your workouts?

Penn: Every day I stretch about half an hour before going to bed. I don't stretch before practice; I just warm up to get the blood going. If I'm not too exhausted, I stretch after training. But often I'll go home, eat, relax, take a shower and then stretch before going to sleep.

A good routine is to start from your head and go down to your feet, stretching everything you want to stretch. Flexibility is essential. That's why so many people have such a hard time taking me down, passing my guard and reversing me when I'm on top. It's important to have strength with your flexibility. At the gym, you often see strong, stiff guys and weak, flexible guys. To become a force in fighting, you need to combine those.

BB: What's an average day like for you when you're preparing for a fight?

Penn: I get to the gym by 6 a.m. and get out by 9 a.m. so I can rest all day, like eight hours straight. Every couple of hours, I eat organic, healthy food—nothing processed. I focus on good carbs, no bad fats, low sodium and two gallons of water a day.

BB: How do you schedule your training around eating that frequently?

Penn: I wake up, drink a shake, go train for two hours, eat an orange to get my insulin level back up, maybe do an hour of cardio, eat again, then just try to stay home. I might wait another two hours until I eat again, or I might come home and eat a cup of brown rice, six egg whites, a chicken breast or something like that. It all depends on the stage of my diet. If I'm trying to drop body fat, it might be a chicken breast in the morning, then tuna and rice with two cups of organic vegetables in the afternoon.

BB: How do you cut weight?

Penn: I just cut down on my food and try to make whatever I eat as healthy as possible. After 6 p.m., I cut the carbs, and then as I start getting closer [to the fight], I eat lighter things like rice and chicken, then maybe just fish and greens at night. Everybody knows: Cut the carbs and cut the fat, and you'll be looking good in no time.

BB: What if you've only got 48 hours to lose several pounds?

Penn: I don't like to do that, but a lot of guys do it. The No. 1 thing: Don't eat anything salty because sodium attracts water weight. Don't use sports drinks for the same reason. The week of the weigh-ins, flush your system by drinking two or three gallons of fresh water every day. You can lose more weight by sitting in the sauna and letting the sweat get all that salt out.

BB: Not many athletes are able to move up and down between weight classes. Why do you do it?

Penn: To me, that's part of what MMA is about. That's especially what jujutsu is about—the little man being able to fight the bigger man.

BB: Do you have any favorite techniques that help you fight bigger men?

Penn: My game has hundreds of moves, and I do all kinds of advanced stuff, but I call what I do "advanced basic." I take the most basic moves and make them as advanced and as strong as possible. For example, if I'm grappling and I'm on bottom, I'm either going to sweep or submit you or stand up. If I'm on my back, I'll try a submission. If that doesn't work, I'll move on to sweep, pass your guard, mount, choke or armbar you. Anything that happens in between those moves, I'll take, but this is the way I try to go every time. When I'm fighting, I come in, punch you, grab you, put you down, pass, mount, choke, armbar. That's the game plan.

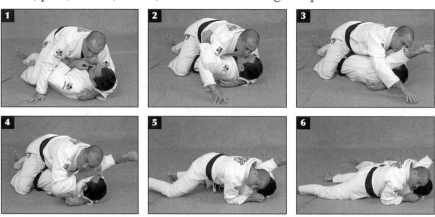

From the mount: B.J. Penn controls his brother, Reagan Penn (1). B.J. "walks" his right hand around his opponent's shoulder (2) and over his head (3) to reposition his left arm. He then uses his right hand and head to push the limb across the opponent's face (4). To finish, the fighter locks his hands (5) and completes the arm triangle (6).

From the open guard: Penn holds his adversary's ankles (1). Before the man can act, Penn flings his legs to the side (2) and executes a punch (3-4). Taking advantage of the man's stunned state, Penn drops into the side-control position (5).

If I'm on my back defending from the guard and you're on top trying to pass or punch me, I'll look for a submission. It could be a triangle or arm lock from my guard, and if I can't get that, I'll look for a sweep to put you on your back. The guy on top controls everything. He controls the weight he's putting on you, and you're constantly pushing him away. Of course, I always want to be on top, but when I'm on bottom, I might try to go for one of the five sweeps I really know. The same thing applies to reversals.

BB: When you're on the ground, do you feel any sense of urgency to win, or do you not worry because you have a great ground game?

Penn: When I'm on my back, I'll go for a couple of moves as quickly as I can. It's not like self-defense, where I can take my time. It's a sad fact of the sport that you're fighting the clock as well as your opponent. It takes away some of the purity of the sport and the martial arts, but that's today's world. You have to be in great shape to push and win.

BB: Which techniques do you think are most effective for MMA?

Penn: You have to learn all the different martial arts if you want to succeed in this sport. The three basic things to learn first are kickboxing, wrestling and jujutsu. You have to build a base and a style so you have something to fall back on in case anything goes wrong in a fight. Your base is your instinct, and you build on it. Jujutsu players add wrestling and kickboxing. If you're a kickboxer, add a good takedown defense and some jujutsu so you don't get submitted easily if you do end up on the ground. Really, it's about making yourself well-rounded—in stand-up, in takedowns and on the ground.

BB: Your base is jujutsu, isn't it?

Penn: I was introduced to it before wrestling. Jujutsu is not the perfect martial art for beating today's high-level UFC athletes, but I still feel that it's one of the best self-defense arts. If you don't want to fight and some guy's trying to punch or kick you, you can still run away. If the guy chases you down and tackles you, you have ground-fighting skills.

Jujutsu's weakness is that a lot of players don't have good takedown defense, which is something you can learn from judo or wrestling.

BB: Which techniques do you find most effective?

Penn: I like to do chokes. Somebody who's caught in an armbar can let his arm break, but if you've got him in a choke, he's going to sleep. If I'm on top and punching you, I might go for an armbar, but most of the time I'm going for a choke.

From your back, you've got to be able to do armbars and triangles, too. With submission skills, you can extend your career. That's why it's important in MMA to save your body and protect your brain. You can win using armbars, locks, slams and takedowns. You don't need to punch each other in the face all day.

BB: Can you sum up your fighting strategy?

Penn: Go straight in and always give a higher output than the other guy. For anything in life, you should just do more than the other guy. No matter how much he does, you do more. Everybody can break, so try to break him mentally. If he throws five punches, you throw 20. If he throws 20, you throw 40. If he defends against 15 takedowns, you do 17. That's just what you have to do every single time you get in there. It's pretty tough to maintain that level, so you'd better be in shape.